IPv6 Primer: *A Concise and Practical Guide for IT Professionals and Students*

Abdul Latiff Esa

John Bires

Tel: 016 2331514 /03-55109630

latiffesa@latiffesa.com

www.latiffesa.com

U. S Copyright 2015

Denial of claims.

Although the publisher has tried his very best to ensure the accuracy of the contents of this book, no guarantess are given be it directly or indirectly. The writer rejects all claims or any liability for any damages due to the contents of this book.

Business and Commercial right

Microsoft and the business logo Windows is the right belonging to Microsoft Corporation. All other business brands and logo that is not mention here is the right belonging to the owner.

ISBN: 978-0-692-39386-4

TABLE OF CONTENTS

ABOUT THE AUTHORS

Abdul Latiff Esa is the most renowned trainer and consultant in Malaysia in the field of computer networking. He was one of the first three IT professionals in Malaysia to become a Microsoft Certified Trainer and is a Certified Network Engineer. He currently holds 40 certifications in his field.

Latiff is well known as a technical trainer, having taught at some of the most prestigious Malaysian technical universities:

- University Malaya
- University Technology Malaysia
- International Islamic University
- University Teknikal Malaysia

He has previously authored 7 Malaysian technical books about computer related subjects:

- TCP/IP and Networking
- Linux Red Hat
- Windows Server 2008
- Windows 7 and Windows Server 2008
- PC Repair and Maintenance
- Windows Server 2003
- Ubuntu Server
- Windows Server 2012
- Cisco Internetworking
- Troubleshooting Network
- Windows 8

Latiff's books are written in a style that is straight to the point and designed to save time for the reader. He's able to write in this style because much of his expertise has been gained through practical experience and field work. He has over 15 years of experience in the field and has completed some very significant projects. He was an instrumental member of the team that redesigned Petronas' network systems for their entire Malaysian operation. He has worked for Cisco Partner as a Technical Consultant. He held the position of Chief Technical Officer for Sepakat, the Malaysian firm that has upgraded and maintained many government systems in Malaysia. Currently, he is the owner of LatiffEsa Technologies, a consulting firm specializing in network design and support and in training IT professionals. You may contact him by email at latiffesa@latiffesa.com or visit his website at **www.latiffesa.com**.

 **John Bires** has over 30 years of experience in engineering and manufacturing, and most importantly, technical writing. He is a Chemical Engineer by training and has developed a broad spectrum of technical knowledge, having worked in 7 industries. He is responsible for the translation of the original text from Malay to English, editing, and for the writing of the front-end of the book.

ACKNOWLEDGEMENTS

The writing of this book has come from the encouragement of Latiff's late father, Esa bin Abdul Rahman. He was also an author, and among other works wrote a book about chess. He was in Latiff's heart as he created this work.

The biggest thanks go to Latiff's students and readers of his previous books for all their great suggestions and recommendations. We've tried to incorporate as many of them as possible in this book.

A special thank you goes to Dan Cogswell for proof reading the book and giving many excellent suggestions for improving its readability.

Lastly, we'd like to thank our immediate and extended families for all their love and support. Especially John's wife, Sabrina Esa Bires.

PREFACE

My passion is teaching. I have logged thousands of hours leading classroom sessions about computer networking and other related subjects. Over the years I have found what works to engage and inspire students to reach the end goal of learning the subject being taught. I am a believer that there are no bad students – only bad teachers!

A book is like a teacher. Some teachers get so mired in the technical details that the student needs toothpicks to keep his eyes open. I have been disappointed that most, and perhaps all, the books that have been written about IPv6 are this way. The average length of an IPv6 book currently in circulation is about 400 pages, and some exceed 900 pages! They are so mired in technical detail that the reader really needs to have a strong understanding of the subject *before* opening the cover; otherwise he will be lost in no time.

A good teacher not only knows his subject, but also knows his students and what works to open their minds. We have written this book with this principle in mind. *IPv6 Primer* is a short introduction to the new internet protocol, written in simple language that most laymen will understand. It uses over 150 illustrations to help the reader in grasping concepts (after all, isn't a picture worth a 1000 words?). Reviews of basic computing concepts are often presented before discussion of the main concept to smooth the flow of learning.

Read and study *IPv6 Primer* FIRST before trying to tackle one of the thick textbooks on the subject. You'll probably find that it will be the only resource you'll need.

Good Learning!

Abdul Latiff Esa

INTRODUCTION

To begin, let's take a step into the future: It's the year 2024 and you are at the grocery store. You didn't make a list of needed items, because grocery lists are now obsolete. Why? Because your refrigerator _knows_ its contents, and it 'talks' to you whenever you want, wherever you are. Most people in 2024 really don't care to understand _how_ the refrigerator knows (a combination of smart packaging and visual recognition tools); they are just grateful for smart refrigerators and packaging and couldn't imagine life without such conveniences. Just like today most of us couldn't imagine life without our smartphones.

The future will be like this. Everything is going to be connected. Every single electronic device you own will communicate with you. If an item has a battery or a wire, you'll be able to access it remotely. Anytime, wherever you are. You'll be able to control everything in your home remotely. Lights. HVAC. Security. You'll know the exact location of your car, even if your son or daughter has borrowed it, and even though you aren't actually _in_ the car, you'll know the fuel level and when it next needs servicing.

Also, the flow of information will be fast! No more waiting for files to download and pages to upload. Information flow will seem almost instantaneous. And these conveniences won't be just for the rich, they will be used by the masses, because connectivity will be cheap.

Those of us that are steeped in the knowledge of computers and networking know that this vision of the future isn't far-fetched. **However, our current internet infrastructure cannot support this vision in its current state.**

So what's wrong with the Internet? It's actually quite simple. It's running out of ..... 'phone numbers'! We'll, not actually phone numbers, but _addresses_. You probably already know that each device that is connected to the internet has an address associated with it. An Internet address is kind of like a phone number, so the internet knows where to call.

Now, the problem with running out of addresses has been going on for a long time, so some workarounds have been implemented to make sure that your device's address doesn't get confused with someone's address on the other side of the world. Other workarounds were implemented to use a single address for multiple devices. Still other workarounds were implemented to compensate for other problems. **All these workarounds have resulted in an Internet that is slower and less efficient and more costly than it could be.**

What's needed to realize the vision of the future is to revise how the internet works, or better said, to revise its _protocol_. Actually, a group of very smart people called the Internet Engineering Task Force have long anticipated these problems and have already developed the new protocol. It's called IPv6 (Internet Protocol, version 6).

IPv6 will replace the current protocol, IPv4. IPv4 is actually the original protocol developed by the US Department of Defense and has been in use ever since the (public) internet was born. It is amazing that for over 25 years IPv4 has been surprisingly appropriate to sustain the growth of the internet; not only the increase in the number of devices connected, but also the kinds of applications and usage that we are inventing every day. This sustainability has been an impressive achievement of engineering excellence.[1]

But now, the world has outgrown IPv4 and needs IPv6 to realize its future.

If you are an IT professional or involved in any way in the development of electrical or electronic devices, you will need at least a basic working knowledge of IPv6. It is the modus operandi of connectivity for the future. And the future will be here in a blink of the eye. This book has been written for you. It is particularly useful for IT professionals that need to 'get the job done' and less useful for those who want to develop an in-depth understanding of the subject (although the later might want to start with this book, before trying to tackle the textbooks). It's also appropriate for college students that are learning how the world connects.

Read **Chapters 1-5** to develop a solid understanding of how addresses are changing and improving with IPv6. **Chapter 6** is all about subnetting, and is particularly useful for the Network designer or Administrator that controls the security of their LAN. **Chapter 7** explains how addresses are reduced to short-

---

[1]_Blanchet, Marc, Migrating to IPv6_, Pg 1, www.ipv6book.ca/doc/ipv6book-chap1.pdf (15Feb2014)

hand in version 6 (v6). **Chapter 8** goes into more depth about how and why physical (equipment) addresses are incorporated into the v6 address. **Chapter 9** is all about error reporting and information messages in v6. **Chapter 10** is all about what happens during boot-up of a device. **Chapter 11** contrasts time-saving dynamic address assignment in v6 vs. v4. **Chapter 12** gives a great short overview of the TCP/IP model, whose understanding is critical to troubleshooting network problems. **Chapter 13** discusses in detail migration to v6 and presents three technologies that can help, with examples. It concludes by showing how to use freeware to simulate migration to v6 before going live. **Appendix A** is a great diagram showing a completed IPv6 network – refer to this diagram frequently as you read the book. **Appendix B** is a 'cheat-sheet' of commands used in Chapter 13 simulations. **Appendix C** is a one-page summary of Ipv6 address blocks and where they are used.

How to use this book: It is suggested that everyone reads the Preface, Introduction and Chapters 1-5. Then you may pick and choose the subsequent chapters that are of interest to you based on the chapter descriptions above. If your goal is to finish with a basic understanding of IPv6 changes and upgrades, you should take the time to read and study the entire book.

GUIDE TO ICONS USED IN THIS BOOK

No	ICON	EXPLANATION
1		COMPUTER
2		SERVER
3		LAYER TWO SWITCH
4		ROUTER
5		LAYER THREE SWITCH
6		ACCESS POINT
7		FIREWALL
8		INTERNET
9		IP PHONE
10	MODE	MODEM
11		WAN CONNECTION
12		CLOUD
13		USERS

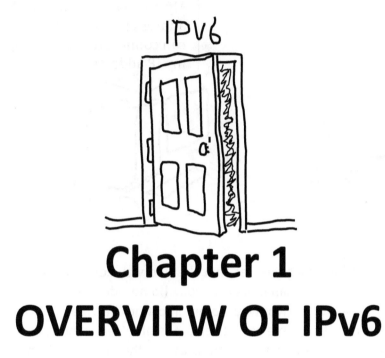

Chapter 1
OVERVIEW OF IPv6

- Introduction to IP Addresses
- A Brief History of Internet Protocols
- Problems with IPv4
- Introduction to IPv6 Addresses
- Advantages of IPv6
- Migrating to IPv6

INTRODUCTION TO IP ADDRESSES

Every device, or _host_, that desires to communicate with another, requires an IP address to do so. It works like the device's phone number. Besides an IP address, each host also requires a hostname as a secondary identity. Both the IP address and the hostname must be unique in order for one host to be able to communicate with another host.

Figure 1

The uniqueness of both identities ensures that the two way communication exists between all hosts. An IP address works the same way as your home address. Just like postal letters use physical addresses to allow a two way communication between two persons located at different locations. It is not possible to deliver a postal letter without an address - the same applies to hosts that will not be able to communicate on the Internet without an IP address.

The illustration above (Figure 1) represents two hosts. One is a notebook computer while the other is a Desktop computer. The notebook computer hostname is LAT with a configured IP address of 2001:db8::1 while the Desktop computer hostname is AL with an IP address of 2001:db8::2. Both the hosts are using a unique hostname and IP address. This allows communication via computer network, given both hosts are connected to the same network.

In a very large organization consisting of hundreds or thousand of hosts, the management of IP address allocation requires proper management. Failure to do so could cause an IP address conflict, where two hosts might be wrongly configured with the same IP address. When this occurs one of the hosts will loose network connectivity. If we were to look at the global scope of the IP address management tasks this would require an organization itself to manage and overlook the IP address assignment.

A BRIEF HISTORY OF INTERNET PROTOCOLS

In the early computer networks, both the TCP (Transmission Control Protocol) and the IP (Internet Protocol) were classified as one protocol, TCP/IP. There were three versions, 1 to 3. When version four was introduced, the protocols were separated into TCP and IP version 4 (IPv4). IPv4 has been in use since the public internet was born, for about the last 25 years. IPv4 superseded other protocols such as IPX/SPX and Netbeui.

IPv5 was developed in the 1970s to overcome the limitations of IPv4 to support voice and video communications over the network. The ST protocol that stands for Internet Stream Protocol was developed with IPv5 to support the needs of voice and video requirements over networks. IPv5 was later abandoned and work on IPv6 started in 1994. IPv6 was not developed from IPv5, instead it was developed based on IPv4.

PROBLEMS WITH IPv4

- **The depletion of IPv4 address.** Back ten years ago the depletion of IPv4 address is one matter that was taken seriously. Though the issue was resolved with the introduction of NAT (Network Address Translation), NAT was a temporary solution and the time would come to face this address shortage issue once again.

- **The problem with NAT.** Although NAT was able to postpone the implementation of IPv6, it has had its own limitations. NAT works by sharing one or multiple public IP addresses by multiple hosts that are using internal LAN private IP addresses. This works fine when used for Internet Connection Sharing, but it limits other technologies from being used across NAT devices. Internal hosts in LAN networks are able to access remote hosts in WAN networks but not vice versa. Some technologies such as VOIP require special handling through the network and are not able to communicate properly. All these issues are overcome with the introduction of IPv6.

Figure 2: Screen capture from a cell phone showing its IP address

The importance and ubiquitousness of the IP address becomes really clear when you realize that one is used on all cell phones today, and that the number of cell phones in use is predicted to exceed the population of the world by 2014![2] The screen capture from a cell phone above (Figure 2) shows its IP address.

---

[2] Pramis, Joshua, *Number of Cell Phones to Exceed World Population by 2014*, Feb 28 2013, Digital Trends, http://www.digitaltrends.com/mobile/mobile-phone-world-population-2014/#!bIpVo8, (Aug 2014)

INTRODUCTION TO IPv6 ADDRESSES

Figure 3 illustrates an example of IPv6 address 2001:0db8:85a3:0042:1000:8a2e:0370:7334 that is separated into 8 bits segments.

1	2	3	4	5	6	7	8	9	10	11	12	13	14	15	16
8	8	8	8	8	8	8	8	8	8	8	8	8	8	8	8
20	01	0d	b8	85	a3	00	42	10	00	8a	2e	03	70	73	34
2001		0db8		85a3		0042		1000		8a2e		0370		7334	
/8	/16	/24	/32	/40	/48	/56	/64	/72	/80	/88	/96	/104	/112	/120	/128

Figure 3: 128 bit IPv6 Address

A clear difference between IPv4 and IPv6 is IPv4 addresses are 32 bits while IPv6 are 128 bits. This comparison is only on the surface. Beyond that actually lie a number of exciting new and future technologies. Here are some more interesting facts about IPv6 addresses:

- The total number of address in IPv4 is 2^32 bits which is equivalent to 4,294,967,296 (4 billion). Whereas the total number of address available in IPv6 is 2^128 bits, which is 340,282,366,920,938,463,463,374,607,431,768,211,456 (340 undecillion, 282 decillion, 366 nonillion, 920 octillion, 938 septillion, 463 sextillion, 463 quintillion, 374 quadrillion, 607 trillion, 431 billion, 768 million, 211 thousand and 456). It is estimated that each person throughout the entire world can be allocated a number of 52 trillion IPv6 address. There are about 7 billion people on our planet earth today.

- It is estimated that there is one billion IPv6 addresses for each square meter on earth including the surface of the sea.

- It is concluded that the shortage of an IPv6 address would only happen in the year of 2400.

ADVANTAGES OF IPv6

- **Humongous amount of addresses available.** The amount of available addresses in IPv4 is so limited compared to IPv6. With so many addresses available in IPv6 it paves the way for the introduction of new technologies, and all existing technologies can be brought online easier at lower costs.

- **Extension header.** The introduction of an extension header allows easy integration with existing and future technologies. It is located between the IPv6 header and the payload (see Figure 4). Unlike IPv4 which uses the option field with a limitation of 40 bytes there is no size limitation being set on IPv6 extension header. It can be arbitrary in length.

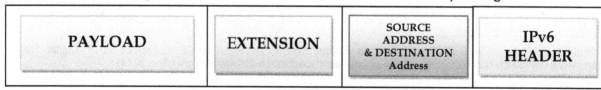

Figure 4

- **Reduced Fragmentation**. Fragmentation is no longer required on intermediary devices such as routers. It is now the responsibility of the transmission host to carry out fragmentation if needed. This simply means increased network performance.

- **Simplified Header.** The IPv6 header has been simplified to reduce the processing overhead on intermediary devices. Although the IPv6 header is twice as large in size as the minimum size of a IPv4 header (40 bytes vs. 20 bytes), the fixed header size of IPv6 has made handling it much easier.

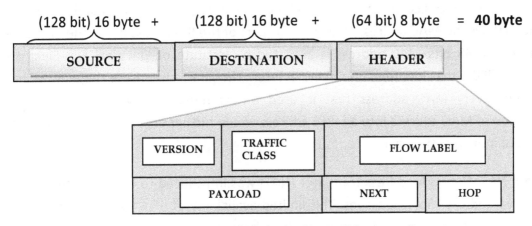

Figure 5: IPv6's Simplified Header

- **Support for flow labeling.** A packet that requires special handling can be labeled and identified and handled accordingly.

- **Support for *authentication* and privacy**. Generally, an IPv4 address allocates 16 bits from the total 32 bits for host bits compared to IPv6 that allocates 64 bits for host bits. This means an attack from a worm virus on IPv6 will take a lot longer to achieve its goal. The two headers that handle security is the **AH** (*Authentication header*) and **ESP** (*Encapsulating Security Payload*) header. AH header secures ***each field*** in the IP header, while ESP secures the header and its payload.

- **Non broadcast.** Broadcast communication that is used in IPv4 is no longer being used in IPv6. Broadcast is not replaced by multicast communication. This will certainly reduce the amount of collision in a network.

- **The first and the last IP address.** Each IPv4 network starts with an IP address identified as a network ID and ends with the last IP address as the broadcast IP address. IPv6 allows each and every address to be used. For example the first IPv6 address for prefix

2001:db8:1234::/64 is 2001:db8:1234:0000:0000:0000:0000:0000/64 and the last address is 2001:db8:1234:0000:ffff:ffff:ffff:ffff/64. Both of these addresses can be configured on a host that requires an IPv6 address. (Note: the nomenclature used above of "/x" means the first "x" bits of the address is fixed. "/64" means the first 64 bits are fixed.)

- **No more ARP**. IPv6 hosts will no longer communicate via address resolution protocol (ARP). ARP is a broadcast at layer two. It is used by IPv4 hosts to locate the MAC address of other hosts. ARP is replaced by network discovery (ND) in IPv6.

- **Stateful and Stateless.** The DHCP (Dynamic Host Configuration Protocol) methodology has been restructured to accommodate a new feature, namely, stateful and stateless. This new method allows the MAC address to be used as part of the IP address itself. The first 24 bits of the entire 48 bits MAC address is allocated by Institute of Electrical and Electronics Engineers (IEEE) that identifies the manufacturer. The goal is to ensure the uniqueness of each and every MAC address that is used on all network devices worldwide. The integration of MAC address into an IPv6 address would further ensure that address conflict issues are a thing of the past.

- **No more NAT.** Network address translator (NAT) was introduced to overcome the problem of the IPv4 address shortage issues. This limited availability of IPv4 addresses certainly led to the increase in price of each and every IP address that there is left. The current rate of renting an IPv4 address is about $100 USD monthly. The huge amount of available addresses in IPv6 simply means that NAT is no longer necessary.

- **IPv6 address allocation for documentation purpose.** Every reference on IPv6 that relates to planning, documentation and discussion is being allocated a reserve IPv6 address of 2001:DB8::/32 according to RFC 3849. These particular addresses are not allowed to be used for any usage other than documentation purpose. The reason for this is to prevent the actual IP addresses from being accidentally exposed to the general public.

MIGRATING TO IPv6

The process of transitioning from IPv4 to IPv6 will take place gradually stage by stage throughout the years. The reason for this is because only the latest hardware and the latest operating systems can fully support the features in IPv6.

THEORETICALLY, the process of transition will start from the proper implementation of the latest IPv6 router that will allocate the prefix to be used as the IPv6 address to client computers. Then it will be followed with the layer three switch that will route communication between vlans. After that, will be the server operating systems and lastly the client computers. The server and client operating systems that fully support IPv6 and take advantage of its capability are currently Windows Server 2008, Windows Server 2012, Windows 7, Windows 8 and Linux.

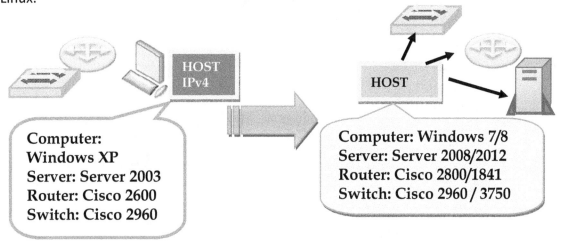

Figure 6: Only the latest hardware and operating systems fully support IPv6

Other systems, such as firewalls, will also need to be replaced with the latest model that support IPv6 with higher flash capacity, larger ram capacity and faster processor, which will certainly be costly. Both the router and firewall will start by supporting both IPv4 and IPv6 protocols communication from the client computers. Every newly purchased computers and network devices should support IPv6 and be backward compatible with IPv4. A router that supports both features will require at least 256 MB of Ram and 64 MB of flash.

IN REALITY, without the public realizing it, the migration process began a few years ago as Windows XP was gradually replaced with Windows Vista and most servers started running Windows Server 2008. Most routers and switches today are also running IPv6, as legacy devices that broke down were replaced with newer models. These new devices were certainly built with larger ram and faster processors to support the increase number of users. Generally we can say that most users are already running Windows 7 or Windows 8 and servers are currently running at least Windows Server 2008 R2. What's left is to configure the existing routers, firewall and layer three switches to support IPv6 and we're done, as easy as that.

Reference
http://www.rfc-editor.org/rfc/rfc6540.txt
https://tools.ietf.org/html/rfc4291
https://tools.ietf.org/html/rfc3513
https://tools.ietf.org/html/rfc6564
https://www.ietf.org/rfc/rfc2460.txt

Chapter 2

HEADER STRUCTURE

- The Structure of IPv6 Headers
- Header comparison IPv6 and IPv4
- IPv6 Header Fields

THE STRUCTURE OF IPv6 HEADERS

You can think of packet headers as being the "shipping labels" pasted on the beginning of all IP data packets. There are significant differences between IPv4 (Figure 7) and IPv6 (Figure 8) as we look into the structure of both headers in detail. IPv6 no longer uses most of the fields that have been part of IPv4 for years. The fields no longer used in IPv6 are:

- Header Length
- Identification
- Fragment Offset
- Flags
- Header Checksum
- Type of Service

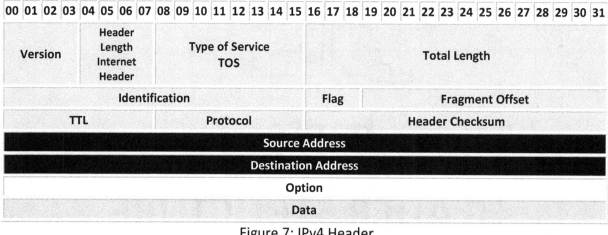

Figure 7: IPv4 Header

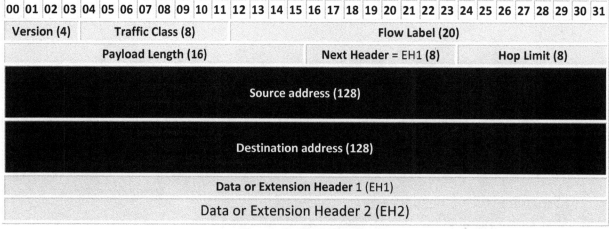

Figure 8: IPv6 Header

DIFFERENCES BETWEEN THE IPv6 and IPv4 HEADER

a. **Header Length**. Due to the fixed size header of IPv6, the header length field is no longer required. In IPv4 header length refers to the option field that is seldom used. This is due to the fact that the option field requires an overall support implementation from source host to the destination host which includes the gateway and the path between communicating hosts. In IPv6 the option field is relocated to the *extension header (EH)* if there is a requirement to use it.

b. **Identification, Fragment Offset and Flags**. These three fields were responsible to handle fragmentation should there be a need to do so by the communicating hosts in IPv4. IPv6 no longer requires it, but instead will make use of Path MTU Discovery. This method called MTU (Maximum Transmission Unit) discovery will identify the correct size of transmission that will best fit the path from source to destination. Therefore the need to fragment on the devices along the path is a thing of the past which will surely reduce the processing overhead on intermediary devices along the path. Should there be a need for such requirement it can be fulfilled by the *extension header (EH)*.

c. **Header checksum**. This field has been removed in IPv6 to reduce the processing overhead on the routers. The reason is that there is no requirement for this when layer two devices are already handling it. Also, the upper layer protocols are already responsible for handling the same tasks, so there is no reason for such tasks to be repeated again and again. This is another reason why IPv6 is surely a network performance enhancer.

d. **Type of Service**. The TOS field was hardly ever used in IPv4 although it has been part of the IP header. This field has been replaced with the Traffic Class field. This field contains information on the special handling requirements of certain type of delay sensitive communication.

e. **Protocol Type**. The Protocol Type field in IPv4 is replaced by the "Next Header" field in IPv6. This field contains information about the upper layer protocols that are required to process the communication between the communicating hosts. Examples are TCP, UDP and ICMP.

f. **Time to Live**. The Time to Live (TTL) field has been replaced by the Hop limit field in IPv6. The time to live field refers to time in millisecond a transmission can stay active in the wire. When the time expires, the transmission will self destruct. This ensures that the network will not be overwhelmed and collisions will be reduced.

IPV6 HEADER FIELDS

One of the main purposes of IPv6 development when compared to IPv4 was to simplify the header. The following will explain each field in the header with reference to Figures 7 & 8.

- **Version (4 bit)**. The Version field refers to the version of IP itself, so it will contain either a four or a six.

- **Traffic Class (8 bit)**. The Traffic Class field is an improvement of the Type of Service field in IPv4. It indicates a transmission that requires special handling so that intermediate devices will be able to differentiate a transmission that requires special handling from one that does not.

- **Flow Label (20 bit).** There are some groups of transmissions that require a different method of handling. Flow label is used to differentiate this type of requirement. The source host will label its transmission so that routers can allocate the required resources to meet its requirement. This will speed up the transmission if there were other groups of transmissions from the same category to avoid repetitive processing.

- **Payload Length (16 bit).** This field refers to the length of data that follows after the IP header. The length does not include the size of the IP header. The size of extension header includes the size of the *payload length*.

- **Next header (8 bit).** The purpose of this field is the same as the Protocol Type field in IPv4. A value of six indicates a TCP protocol type, whereas 17 is a UDP protocol type. The Next Header field refers to the extension header that is between the IP header and TCP or UDP header.

- **Hop Limit (8 bit).** This field serves the same purpose as the TTL field used in IPv4. It represents the number of network segments on which the packet is allowed to travel before being discarded by a router. The Hop Limit is set by the sending host (max value of $2^8=256$) and is used to prevent packets from endlessly circulating on an IPv6 network. When forwarding a packet, IPv6 routers are required to decrease the Hop Limit by 1 and to discard the packet when 0 is reached.

- **Source Address (128 bit).** This field contains information about the transmitting host IP address.

- **Destination Address (128 bit).** This field contains the receiving hosts IPv6 address.

- **Extension Header (Data).** The EH field replaces the Identification field, Fragment Offset and Flags and Header Length from IPv4. As an example, the EH field may contain information regarding the size of the entire transmission that has been fragmented so that the receiving hosts can properly assemble the fragment accordingly.

Reference
https://tools.ietf.org/html/rfc6282
https://tools.ietf.org/html/rfc6564
https://tools.ietf.org/html/rfc791
https://www.rfc-editor.org/rfc/rfc4302.txt

Chapter 3
ADDRESS FORMAT

- IANA, RIR and ISP
- Compressing IPv6 Addresses
- IPv6 Prefix Format

IANA, RIR, and ISP

Internet Assigned Numbers Authority (IANA) is an organization in the United States that is responsible to manage and allocate the assignment of IPv6 addresses. IANA then assigns the branch of the Regional Internet Registry (RIR) to manage the same task with a smaller scale according to regions such as APNIC for Asia pacific and ARIN for the United States, Canada, Antarctica and several parts of Caribbean region.

Figure 9A indicates the address allocation for IPv6 addresses to several blocks. Addresses beginning with 001 are classified as Global Unicast Addresses. RIR will allocate Global Unicast Addresses from within their scope. RIR manages the allocation of IPv6 addresses. For example, each country that is in the Asia Pacific will fall under the management of Asia-Pacific Network Information Centre (APNIC) that is based in Brisbane Australia.

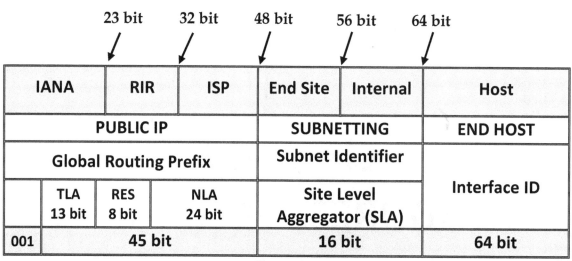

Figure 9A

IANA allocates blocks of addresses to RIR who will subdivide the block of addresses to individual ISP. The ISP then allocates public IPv6 addresses to local organization and end users. As at of this writing the allocation block to each RIR is /23 ("/23" means the first 23 bits). RIR then allocates the /32 block to ISPs in each country who then assigns the prefix of /48 to /56 to its customers. That means end users and organizations will make use bits 49 to 64 or bits 57 to 64 for subnetting purposes according to its network requirement. Development, discussions and allocations of IPv6 addresses will continue to change now and then to better fulfill the requirement of users, and existing and new technologies. Discussions related to subnetting continue to be debated in a lot of IPv6 forums. There is a debate on whether the use of /127 or /64 is the most suitable for point to point WAN connections. At the moment, IPv4 makes use of /30 for the purpose of point to point connection. Most recommendations suggest a prefix of /64 should be used for each and every purpose of address assignment to IPv6 hosts. There is also a suggestion that point to point connections should be allocated with a prefix of /64 which allows the flexibility to use the prefix of /127 should the need arise. There will be further explanation on this in the upcoming chapters.

	ID	BITS	EXPLANATION
1	FP	3	Format Prefix (001)
2	TLA	13	• Top Level Aggregator. IANA will determine the value of TLA that will be allocated to RIR (Regional Internet Registry).
3	RES	8	• Reserved for future use
4	NLA	24	• Next Level Aggregator. This is the value that will be allocated by TLA or RIR to its ISP. The ISP that's been allocated this value will than have to manage the SLA.
5	SLA	16	• Site Level Aggregator. This is the value allocated by ISP to organizations or end users.
6	INTERFACE	64	• Interface Identifier. This is the value of for each host.

Figure 9B

Referring to Figure 9A and 9B, the first three bits that is 001 refers to the global unicast address. The first forty eight bits represents the topology that is categorized as public network. The next sixteen bits represents the topology that is categorized as site.

TLA (Top Level Aggregator) is at the highest level from the scope of *routing hierarchy*. The eight bits categorized under RES is reserved for future technologies. NLA is the value being allocated to ISP for the country by TLA to manage the allocation of SLA to each site that requires it. TLA ID is the address prefix for RIR that will manage the allocation for Internet Service Provider (ISP) for each country. As of this writing, the TLA that is responsible to manage the allocation to ISPs in Malaysia is APNIC (Asia Pacific Network Information Centre) that is based in Brisbane, Australia.

SLA (Site Level Aggregator) is the address that is that is allocated to end users or organizations by NLA. Organizations of networks located throughout each country will manage its SLA according to its own requirements. Subnet is derived from the allocated value of SLA. The sixteen bits of SLA can support up to 65,535 subnets.

COMPRESSING THE IPv6 ADDRESS
The IPv6 address is very long compared to the all very familiar IPv4 address that we are so used to. To make things much easier for everyone two user friendly methods of compressing IPv6 addresses were introduced. The first method is *zero compression* and the second is *leading zero compression*. The following figure explains:

COMPRESSING IPv6 ADDRESSES		
1	::	• **Zero compression** allows 2 or more contiguous 16-bit blocks of zeros to be summarised as ":". Note: ":" can only be used once in an address (otherwise you couldn't tell which blocks were compressed)
	1041:0:130B:**0000:0000**:9C0:586C:1305	• Compressed as: 1041:0:130B : :9C0:586C:1305.
2	2001:**0**db8:abcd:**0**123::9	• **Leading zero** allows leading zeros to be dropped. This method can be repeated for each block there is. The rule also implies that there should be at least one value in the block. The value can be a zero or any value at all.
		• Compressed: 2001:db8:abcd:123::9
	2001:**0**db8:**0000:000**3::9	• Compressed: 2001:db8:0:3::9
3	1050:0000:0000:0000:0005:0600:300c:326b	• 1050:0:0:0:5:600:300c:326b
4	ff06:0:0:0:0:0:0:c3	• ff06::c3
5	0:0:0:0:0:ffff:192.1.56.10	• ::ffff:192.1.56.10/96 . Ipv4 mapped Ipv6
6	0:0:0:0:0:0:192.1.56.10	• ::192.1.56.10/96. Ipv4 compatible Ipv6
7	FF02:0:0:0:0:0:0:2	• FF02::2.
8	FF02:30:0:0:0:0:0:5	• FF02:30::5
9	FE80:0:0:0:2AA:FF:FE9A:4CA2	• FE80::2AA:FF:FE9A:4CA2

Figure 10: examples of address compression

IPV6 PREFIX FORMAT

The *prefix* is the left-most part of an IPv6 address that identifies the network; the rest of the address specifies particular addresses in that network. Thus all the addresses in one network have the same first N bits. The notation of "/N" is used to denote a prefix N bits long. For example, this is how the network containing all addresses that begin with the 32 bits "2001:0db8" is written as 2001:db8::/32. This notation is used whenever we are talking about a whole network, and don't care about the individual addresses in it. Prefixes are used for routing and subnet identifiers like Classless Inter-Domain Routing (CIDR) notation does for IPv4. The prefix is like an IPv4 subnet mask.

Reference
https://tools.ietf.org/html/rfc4291
https://tools.ietf.org/html/rfc3177
https://tools.ietf.org/html/rfc3769
https://tools.ietf.org/html/rfc4147
https://www.iana.org/numbers
http://www.ietf.org/rfc/rfc4029.txt

Chapter 4
TYPES OF ADDRESSES

- Introduction: A Brief Comparison of IPv4 Vs IPv6
- IPv6 Address Types:
    1. Unicast
        a. Global Unicast
        b. Link Local
        c. Site Local
        d. Unique Local
    2. Multicast
    3. Anycast
    4. Special Addresses
        1. Unspecified
        2. Compatibility
            i. IPv4 mapped Ipv6
            ii. IPv4 compatible IPv6
        3. Loopback
        4. Temporary Addresses
        5. Documentation Addresses

INTRODUCTION: A Brief Comparison of IPv4 Vs IPv6 Address Types

There's many differences in the way addressing is done in IPv6 vs. IPv4. Figure 11 gives a brief comparison. The remainder of this chapter will detail and contrast these differences.

COMPARING IPv4 WITH IPv6	
IPv4	**IPv6**
Multicast **224.0.0.0 – 239.255.255.255**	Multicast **ff00:: – ff0f::/8**
Broadcast **255.255.255.255**	Broadcast no longer used. It is replaced with Multicast **FF02::1**
Unspecified address **0.0.0.0**	Unspecified is **::**
Loopback **127.0.0.1**	Loopback **::1**
Public IP address	Global Unicast address
Private IP block **10.0.0.0/8, 172.16.0.0/12, 192.168.0.0/16**	Unique Local Address **FC00::/48 dan FD00::/48**
APIPA Address **169.254.0.0/16**	Link Local Address **FE80::/64**
Dotted Decimal	Colon Hexadecimal
Network refers to the value of Subnet Mask.	Network refers to prefix length notation.

Figure 11: Brief Contrast of Addressing in IPv4 vs. IPv6

IPv6 ADDRESS CLASSES

The three main address types for IPv6 are:
1. Unicast
   a. Global unicast address (GUA)
   b. Link-local address (LLA)
   c. Site-local address (SLA)
   d. Unique-local address (ULA)
2. Multicast
3. Anycast

In addition, IPv6 has special addresses such as the loopback address:

4. Special addresses

Unlike IPv4, IPv6 does not make use of address classes to categorize ranges of hosts.

1. **UNICAST:** ONE TO ONE Communication is a type of one-host to another-host communication. Unicast address refers to the address of an interface, like Local Area Connection for Windows operating systems, *interface* eth0 for Linux operating systems, or gigaethernet 0/0 that refers to a router *interface*. Unicast communication is a communication from one interface to another; that is from one source *interface* to another destination *interface*. The following lists the several types of unicast.

- a. Global Unicast addresses (GUA)
- b. Link-local addresses (LLA)
- c. Site-local addresses (SLA)
- d. Unique-local Address (ULA)

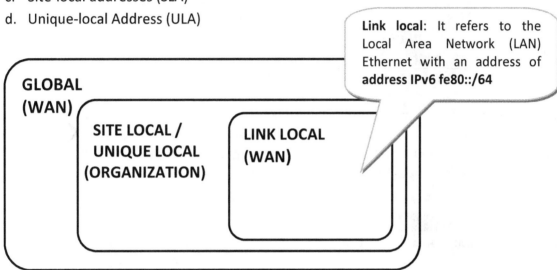

Figure 12: Types of Unicast Addresses

1a. GLOBAL UNICAST ADDRESS (GUA) 2000::/3

The purpose of global unicast addresses is for global routing, which is the same as public IP addresses with IPv4. It is unique globally. The main goal of the global aggregatable address is to lessen the processing overhead on ISP routers by reducing the size of the routing entry inside the routing table of the router. An ISP router may contain up to several hundred bits of routing entry. The "Most Significant Bits" of global unicast address of TLA, NLA and SLA is also classified as global routing prefix and subnet identifier. Refer to Figures 13A and B.

IPv6 GLOBAL UNICAST ADDRESS															
1	2	3	4	5	6	7	8	9	10	11	12	13	14	15	16
8 bit	8 bit	8 bit	8 bit	8 bit	8 bit	8 bit	8 bit	8 bit	8 bit	8 bit	8 bit	8 bit	8 bit	8 bit	8 bit
20	01	0d	b8	85	a3	00	42	10	00	8a	2e	03	70	73	34
2001		0db8		85a3		0042		1000		8a2e		0370		7334	
/8	/16	/24	/32	/40	/48	/56	/64	/72	/80	/88	/96	/104	/112	/120	/128
ROUTING PURPOSE						SUBNET		IDENTIFY HOST							
GLOBAL ROUTING						SUBNET ID		INTERFACE ID							
NETWORK PORTION								HOST PORTION							

48 bit		16 bit	64 bit
3 bit	45 bit	16 bit	64 bit

Figure 13A

IPv6 GLOBAL UNICAST ADDRESS															
1								2							
1	2	3	4	5	6	7	8	1	2	3	4	5	6	7	8
2				0				0				1			
8	4	2	1	8	4	2	1	8	4	2	1	8	4	2	1
0	0	1	0	0	0	0	0	0	0	0	0	0	0	0	1
GLOBAL UNICAST 3 bit			GLOBAL ROUTING PREFIX /45 to /48												

Figure 13B (detail of first two 8-bit segments from 13A)

The first three bits of a global address is binary 001 with a prefix of /3. This means that any bit combination can be used after that first three bits, for example 2000(**0010**), 2001(0010) and 3000(**0011**), but NOT 4000 (0100). As at of this writing IANA has allocated 2000::/3 for global unicast addresses according to RFC 4291. Figure 14 illustrates this:

BIT	1	2	3	4	5	6	7	8	9	10	11	12	13	14	15	16	
BINARY	0	0	1	0	0	0	0	0	0	0	0	0	0	0	0	0	/3
NILAI	8	4	2	1	8	4	2	1	8	4	2	1	8	4	2	1	
IPV6	2				0				0				0				2000::/3

Figure 14

Figure 15 is the breakdown of the IPv6 address 2001::/3

BIT	1	2	3	4	5	6	7	8	9	10	11	12	13	14	15	16	
BINARY	0	0	1	0	0	0	0	0	0	0	0	0	0	0	0	1	/3
NILAI	8	4	2	1	8	4	2	1	8	4	2	1	8	4	2	1	
IPV6	2				0				0				1				2001::/3

Figure 15

Referring again to Figures 13A, _Interface ID_ is part of the IPv6 address that identifies a host. Each physical interface can have several interface IDs. An allocation of sixty four bits for _interface_ ID is taken up in bits 65 through 128. The interface ID is the host identity at layer two, the data link layer.

(Again referring to Figure 13A), _Subnet ID:_ An allocation of sixteen bits for subnetting will give a total of 65,536 subnets. This is kept in bits 49 through 64. Although this huge number seems like a waste of IP addresses, its advantage is the ease of IP address management, administration and designing new networks.

There are three categories of IPv6 global Unicast addresses that will be requested by public users from the ISP:

1. An allocation of prefix /128 will be allocated to users that requests only one IPv6 address. A prefix of /128 means that there will only be one address in that particular network (which is unlikely).
2. If the need only requires one subnet, a prefix of /64 will be allocated.
3. If the request is for a network to support a substantial number of hosts, typically a prefix of /48 will be allocated. Smaller networks could be allocated between /58 to /64

1b. LINK LOCAL ADDRESS (LLA) FE80::/10

The address block fe80::/10 has been reserved for link-local unicast addressing. The allocation of IPv6 Link Local Address starts from FE80:: and ends at FEBF:: (the value right before FEC0). The IPv6 link local address serves almost the same purpose as how APIPA (Automatic Private IP Addressing-169.254.Y.Z) does in IPv4.

APIPA was introduced by Microsoft with Windows 98.) The link local address will be activated by the host computer once IPv6 is enabled. This happens even in situations where there is no unicast address configured. The LLA allows hosts that fall under the same link local network to communicate with each other. An example of a link local address is fe80::250:b6ff:fe01:cfda, shown in Figures 16A and B.

The difference between APIPA and LLA is that APIPA will only be activated on DHCP clients that fail to obtain an address from DHCP servers while LLA is activated on all interfaces in every situation. The last sixty four bit value is the physical address of the interface. The LLA is prohibited WAN connections. LLA should not used as routing for LAN and WAN networks. Networks that are using LLA alone will not be able to connect to the Internet.

BIT	1	2	3	4	5	6	7	8	9	10	11	12	13	14	15	16	/10
BINARY	1	1	1	1	1	1	1	0	1	0	0	0	0	0	0	0	
NILAI	8	4	2	1	8	4	2	1	8	4	2	1	8	4	2	1	
IPv6	F				E				8				0				FE80::/10

Figure 16B (detail of first two 8-bit segments from 16A)

IPv6 LINK LOCAL ADDRESS															
1	2	3	4	5	6	7	8	9	10	11	12	13	14	15	16
8 bit	8 bit	8 bit	8 bit	8 bit	8 bit	8 bit	8 bit	8 bit	8 bit	8 bit	8 bit	8 bit	8 bit	8 bit	8 bit
FE	80	00	00	00	00	00	00	02	50	B6	FF	FE	01	CF	DA
FE80		0000		0000		0000		250		B6FF		FE01		CFDA	
/8	/16	/24	/32	/40	/48	/56	/64	/72	/80	/88	/96	/104	/112	/120	/128
								INTERFACE ID							
NETWORK								HOST							
48 bit						16 bit		64 bit							
10 bit	54 bit (All 0 bits)							64 bit							

Figure 16A

LLA is used for Neighbor Discovery communication, using the ICMPv6 protocol type 135 (neighbor solicitation) and 136 (neighbor advertisement), replacing the ARP communication in IPv4. The goal is to obtain the MAC address of other hosts in the same network.

Operating Systems such as Windows XP and Windows Server 2003 will make use of its physical address for the last sixty four bits of the IPv6 address. Newer operating systems such as Windows 8 will make use of a random *interface* ID (non EUI-64 base *interface* ID) for the same purpose. Figure 17 shows a *physical address* of 00-23-4e-78-55-d4 with an LLA address of fe80::6dd8:9388:dd30:8ae0.

```
Wireless LAN adapter Wireless Network Connection:

   Connection-specific DNS Suffix  . : Home
   Description . . . . . . . . . . . : Atheros AR5007EG Wireless Network Adapter

   Physical Address. . . . . . . . . : 00-23-4E-78-55-D4
   DHCP Enabled. . . . . . . . . . . : Yes
   Autoconfiguration Enabled . . . . : Yes
   Link-local IPv6 Address . . . . . : fe80::6dd8:9388:dd30:8ae0%12(Preferred)
   IPv4 Address. . . . . . . . . . . : 192.168.2.201(Preferred)
```

Figure 17: Newer operating systems assign a random interface ID

Neighbor Discovery communication is also used to avoid IP address conflicts. By default, the Link Local Address will not be routed. It will not be processed by any router. LLA (FE80) is a priority address for link local communication. Hosts located on the same network will use the LLA for communication among them.

Figure 18 shows a router configuration that configures its interface fa0/1 to make an IPv6 address of 2001:db8:0:15::1/64. Interface fa0/0 was made active, but without any IPv6 address configured on it. Interface fa0/0 automatically activates the link local address of fe80::202:17ef:fec1:701 while the address of link local for interface fa0/1 is fe80::202:17ef:fec1:702. Both link local addresses were made active by the router when the IPv6 address of 2001 configuration was configured on 0/1 and when IPv6 was enabled on interface fa0/0.

Figure 18: router configuration

```
latiffesa(config)#int fa0/1
latiffesa(config-if)#ipv6 address 2001:db8:0:15::1/64
latiffesa(config-if)#int fa0/0
latiffesa(config-if)#ipv6 enable
latiffesa(config-if)#do show ipv6 interface brief
FastEthernet0/0           [administratively down/down]
    FE80::202:17FF:FEC1:701
FastEthernet0/1           [administratively down/down]
    FE80::202:17FF:FEC1:702
    2001:DB8:0:15::1
```

ZONE IDENTIFIER (SCOPE ID/ZONE ID): Figure 19 shows an IPv6 address of fe80:5c10:b9f1:b33f:689a for the Local Area Connection and fe80::f426:3901:cfc4:2b49 for the Wireless Network Connection on Windows 7 operating systems.

Figure 19

```
Wireless LAN adapter Wireless Network Connection:

    Connection-specific DNS Suffix  . : Home
    Link-local IPv6 Address . . . . . : fe80::f426:3901:cfc4:2b49%11
    IPv4 Address. . . . . . . . . . . : 192.168.2.201
    Subnet Mask . . . . . . . . . . . : 255.255.255.0
    Default Gateway . . . . . . . . . : 192.168.2.200

Ethernet adapter Local Area Connection:

    Connection-specific DNS Suffix  . : Home
    IPv6 Address. . . . . . . . . . . : fc00:1234:5678:9abc::2
    Link-local IPv6 Address . . . . . : fe80::5c10:b9f1:b33f:689a%10
    IPv4 Address. . . . . . . . . . . : 192.168.2.206
    Subnet Mask . . . . . . . . . . . : 255.255.255.0
    Default Gateway . . . . . . . . . : 192.168.2.200
```

The Character "%" that appears after IPv6 address is used to separate the IP address from the zone ID. In Figure 19, the Characters *%11* and *%10* that appear after the IPv6 addresses of fe80::f426:3901: cfc4:2b49 *% 11* and fe80:5c10:b9F1:b33f:689a *% 10* are used to separate the IP address from the zone ID. It is in the format of *IPv6Address%zoneID*. The purpose of zone ID is to allow the local host to differentiate its own interface to another. A host may have more than one interface. For example most hosts today will have one Local Area Connection interface and one Wireless Connection interface. The figure shows that our host has two interfaces with both allocated a zone ID. The interfaces shown are "*Wireless lan adapter wireless network connection*" and "*ethernet adapter local area connection*" In such a situation the hosts will generate two local link addresses.

1c. SITE LOCAL ADDRESS (SLA) FEC0::/10

The address block fec0::/10 has been reserved for site-local Unicast addressing. A Site Local Address is similar to a private IPv4 address. In IPv4, a private IP address would not be routable on the Internet. The private addresses are IPv4 blocks of 10.0.0.0/8, 172.16.0.0/12, and 192.168.0.0/16.

IPv6 SITE LOCAL ADDRESS															
1	2	3	4	5	6	7	8	9	10	11	12	13	14	15	16
8 bit	8 bit	8 bit	8 bit	8 bit	8 bit	8 bit	8 bit	8 bit	8 bit	8 bit	8 bit	8 bit	8 bit	8 bit	8 bit
FE	C0	00	00	00	00	00	00	02	02	17	FF	FE	C1	07	01
FEC0		0000		0000		0000		202		17FF		FEC1		701	
/8	/16	/24	/32	/40	/48	/56	/64	/72	/80	/88	/96	/104	/112	/120	/128
48 bit						16 bit		64 bit (HOST)							

Figure 20A: Example of a site-local address

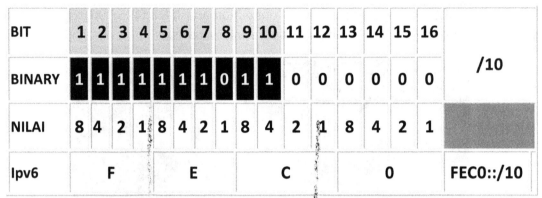

BIT	1	2	3	4	5	6	7	8	9	10	11	12	13	14	15	16	/10
BINARY	1	1	1	1	1	1	1	0	1	1	0	0	0	0	0	0	
NILAI	8	4	2	1	8	4	2	1	8	4	2	1	8	4	2	1	
Ipv6	F		E		C				0								FEC0::/10

Figure 20B: (detail of first two 8-bit segments from 20A)

While LLAs limit the host's communication to the Local Area Network, SLAs limit communication to the site. The current status of site local address is "deprecated" as documented in RFC 3879. Routers by default will limit the communication of SLA within LAN networks only. IPv6 Address FEC0, FED0, FEE0 and FEF0 are categorized as site local address.

1d. UNIQUE LOCAL ADDRESS FC00::/7

Information on Unique Local Address (ULA) is documented in RFC 4193. ULA was introduced to replace site local address (RFC 1884), but can be used for communication within site and between sites. Addresses categorized under ULA cannot be used for routing across the Internet.

Figure 21 shows a ULA being broken into binary and hex. Rather than being dot separated octets, it is in double octet format separated by colons. Highlighted in the first two columns, the 16 bit value is where the ULA address should be subnetted for routing within a site. If a device is configured only with ULA without GUA, such device is considered having a certain level of security since it will not be accessible from the Internet.

IPv6 UNIQUE LOCAL ADDRESS															
1	2	3	4	5	6	7	8	9	10	11	12	13	14	15	16
8 bit	8 bit	8 bit	8 bit	8 bit	8 bit	8 bit	8 bit	8 bit	8 bit	8 bit	8 bit	8 bit	8 bit	8 bit	8 bit
FC	00	53	5B	82	E4	00	00	00	00	00	00	00	00	00	53
FC00		535B		82E4		0000		0000		0000		0000		0053	
/8	/16	/24	/32	/40	/48	/56	/64	/72	/80	/88	/96	/104	/112	/120	/128
								INTERFACE ID							
8	40 bit - RANDOM					16 bit		64 bit							

Figure 21: Example of an ULA

The 8th bit, is also know as the "*L*" bit. A value of 0 indicates that the address is globally assigned; a value of 1 indicates the address is locally assigned – see Figures 22A & B.

BIT	1	2	3	4	5	6	7	8	9	10	11	12	13	14	15	16	
BINARY	1	1	1	1	1	1	0	0	0	0	0	0	0	0	0	0	/7
NILAI	8	4	2	1	8	4	2	1	8	4	2	1	8	4	2	1	
IPV6	F			C			0				0						FC00::/8

Figure 22A: When the 8th bit is 0, the address is <u>globally</u> assigned.

BIT	1	2	3	4	5	6	7	8	9	10	11	12	13	14	15	16	
BINARY	1	1	1	1	1	1	0	1	0	0	0	0	0	0	0	0	/7
NILAI	8	4	2	1	8	4	2	1	8	4	2	1	8	4	2	1	
IPv6	F			D			0				0						FD00::/8

Figure 22B: When the 8th bit is 1, the address is <u>locally</u> assigned.

Note that bits 1 through 8 can now become either FC00 or FD00. Figure 23 shows how each is used:

ULA – UNIQUE LOCAL ADDRESS			
RFC4193 **FC00::/7** (Replaces FEC0/10)	**FC00::/8** 11111100	L bit is 0	• **GLOBALLY ASSIGNED** or centrally assigned. As of this writing, there is no *authority* or registrar that is responsible to manage. The main purpose of globally assigned is to ensure the uniqueness of the address. • This usage would fulfill the requirement of large organizations with branch offices that require connectivity and at the same time want to avoid IP address conflicts. • It will not be included in the global IPv6 routing table. • The plan is to implement a one time minimal charge of its assignment to users without any subsequent charges. • Current status is *dormant*.
	FD00::/8 11111101	L Bit is 1	• **LOCALLY ASSIGNED**. The usage would not guarantee the address uniqueness. • The usage would fulfill the requirement of small

			disconnected sites. Disconnected from the Internet. • Without AAAA or PTR DNS. • No registrar was appointed to manage the allocation of this address block. It should be managed by the network administrator's own discretion. The forty bit value is random. Refer to Figure 24. • There will be no charges for its usage. • Current status is *dormant*.

Figure 23: Explanation of the "L" bit summarized

Figure 24 shows what has been discussed in this section as part of the entire 128 bit address:

FC00::/7				
128 bit				
/48				64 bit
/64				64 bit
7 bit	1 bit	40 bit	16 bit	64 bit
/7	BIT 0 (GLOBAL) or BIT 1 (LOCAL)	Random, non contiguous, non globally routable.	/16	/64
PREFIX	L FLAG	GLOBAL ID	SUBNET ID	INTERFACE ID

Figure 24: "L" bit shown in zoom-out view in the entire 128 bit address

Just as SLA replaces the private IPv4 address, ULA replaces SLA. This means that ULA also serves the same purpose of private IP addresses in IPv4. We can conclude that ULA will be used for temporary communication within and across sites. At a later stage there is the possibility that this network will be connected to the Internet, and when this happens GUA will replace ULA.

Another purpose of ULA is to allow VPN communication across sites. Filtering on ULA FC00 should reflect and limit its communication within and between sites.

Figure 25 shows a Microsoft operating system configured with an ULA of FC00 and Figure 26 is a hardware router being enabled with a SLA of FEC0 (deprecated). On a router the same method of configuration can be done to enable a ULA. Notice that in Figure 25 when a device is enabled with the IPv6 protocol, it will immediately generate an LLA and possibly with a ULA too if the local network infrastructure has been configured an allocation to assign ULA prefix to hosts.

```
Ethernet adapter Local Area Connection:

   Connection-specific DNS Suffix  . : Home
   Description . . . . . . . . . . . : Intel(R) 82577LM Gigabit Network Connecti
on
   Physical Address. . . . . . . . . : F0-DE-F1-32-8F-D4
   DHCP Enabled. . . . . . . . . . . : Yes
   Autoconfiguration Enabled . . . . : Yes
   IPv6 Address. . . . . . . . . . . : fc00:1234:5678:9abc::2(Preferred)
   Link-local IPv6 Address . . . . . : fe80::5c10:b9f1:b33f:689a%10(Preferred)
   IPv4 Address. . . . . . . . . . . : 192.168.2.206(Preferred)
   Subnet Mask . . . . . . . . . . . : 255.255.255.0
   Lease Obtained. . . . . . . . . . : Sunday, 10 February, 2013 3:38:23 PM
   Lease Expires . . . . . . . . . . : Monday, 11 February, 2013 3:38:22 PM
   Default Gateway . . . . . . . . . : 192.168.2.200
   DHCP Server . . . . . . . . . . . : 192.168.2.200
```

Figure 25: A Windows operating system configured with the FC00 ULA and FE80 LLA

```
latiffesa(config)#int fa0/0
latiffesa(config-if)#ipv6 address FEC0::/64 eui-64
latiffesa(config-if)#do show ipv6 interface brief
FastEthernet0/0                [administratively down/down]
    FE80::201:63FF:FE43:D401
    FEC0::201:63FF:FE43:D401
```

Figure 26: A router configured with the FC00 ULA and FE80 LLA

2. MULTICAST FF00::/8

The allocation of multicast addresses starts from FF00:: to FF0F:: . This means that all eight high order bits are 1, that is: 11111111. Refer to Figure 27B. The next three bits are all zero, and the bit after that is called the "T" bit, which can have a value of either one or zero.

IPv6 MULTICAST ADDRESS															
1	2	3	4	5	6	7	8	9	10	11	12	13	14	15	16
8 bit	8 bit	8 bit	8 bit	8 bit	8 bit	8 bit	8 bit	8 bit	8 bit	8 bit	8 bit	8 bit	8 bit	8 bit	8 bit
FF	0E														
FF0E		0		0		0		0		0		0		101	
16 bit		112 bit													
		GROUP MULTICAST ID													
/8	/16	/24	/32	/40	/48	/56	/64	/72	/80	/88	/96	/104	/112	/120	/128
Note: This multicast address destination is to all NTP server on the Internet															

Figure 27A: A Multicast Address

MULTICAST															
1								2							
1	2	3	4	5	6	7	8	1	2	3	4	5	6	7	8
F				F				0				E			
8	4	2	1	8	4	2	1	8	4	2	1	8	4	2	1
1	1	1	1	1	1	1	1	0	0	0	T	1	1	1	0
MULTICAST								Reserved				SCOPE ID			
								FLAG							

Figure 27B: (detail of first two 8-bit segments from 27A)

If the value of the T bit is one, then it is a "well known" multicast. This type of multicast is an Internet Assigned Numbers Authority (IANA) assigned value that is allocated for a specific purpose. Figures 29 and 30 detail these specific purposes.

T	T BIT EXPLANATION
0	This is a Multicast address that is categorised as well know and is permanently assigned.
1	This identifies a Multicast address that is categorized as temporarily assigned or locally generated.

Figure 28: The "T" bit determines the type of Multicast Address

SCOPE ID			MULTICAST ADDRESS SCOPE
0000	0	FFx0::/16	Reserve.
0001	1	FFX1::/16	**Interface local.** This is a multicast that is limited to the local host only. It is like loopback multicast.
0010	2	FFX2::/16	**Link Local.** This type of multicast will not be processed by a router. It will remain in the scope of the LAN only. It will not be routed.
0011	3	FFX3::/16	**Subnet local.** This type of multicast makes communication among the hosts on different subnets across multiple links possible. The scope is larger than of link local.
0100	4	FFX4::/16	**Admin local.** It is the smallest scope of multicast and requires manual configuration.
0101	5	FFX5::/16	**Site Local.** This type of multicast is limited to the site local scope. It is restricted to the local physical

			network.
1000	8	FFX8::/16	**Organizational local**. The type of multicast is limited to the organization scope only. An example will be a VPN connectivity that encapsulates it inside another protocol.
1110	E	FFXe::/16	**Global**. A global multicast that traverse the public Internet connection.

Figure 29: IANA assigned ranges

MULTICAST	EXPLANATION
FF01:0:0:0:0:0:0:1	All node in the scope of node local.
FF01:0:0:0:0:0:0:2	All router in the scope of node local.
FF02:0:0:0:0:0:0:1	All node in the scope of link local.
FF02:0:0:0:0:0:0:2	All router in the scope of link local.
FF02:0:0:0:0:0:0:5	All OSPFv3 router in the scope of link local.
FF02:0:0:0:0:0:0:6	All OSPFv3 Designated router in the scope of link local.
FF02:0:0:0:0:0:0:9	All RIPng router in the scope of link local.
FF02:0:0:0:0:0:0:A	All EIGRP router in the scope of link local.
FF02:0:0:0:0:0:1:2	All DHCP server and relay in the scope of link local.
FF02:0:0:0:0:0:0:16	Allows the IPv6 router in the scope of link local to locate the existence of multicast listeners. It also allows to identify differentiation among the various categories of host multicast that is happening in the local link.
FF05:0:0:0:0:0:0:2	All IPv6 router in the scope of site local.

Figure 30: Examples of permanently assigned addresses. The broadcast communication sent by an IPv4 host is received by every host. Each and every host then needs to process the broadcast received and determine if the broadcast received is meant for the host. Multicast in IPv6 is meant to replace the broadcast communication in IPv4. Figure 31 shows that an IPv6 address is configured on a router interface fastethernet 0/0 with an IPv6 address of 2001:1::/64 eui-64. Figure 32 shows that the router had joined the multicast group of FF02::1 and FF02::2. This means that this router had joined the all node multicast group in the scope of link local and all router in the scope of link local. Once a router is configured an IPv6 address it will automatically join a multicast group. IPv6 forwarding is disabled by default on a router. The command *ipv6 unicast-routing* will activate IPv6 forwarding features. The "joined group address" is a clear statement that the router is in a multicast group.

```
latiffesa(config)#ipv6 unicast-routing
latiffesa(config)#int fa0/0
latiffesa(config-if)#ipv6 address 2001:1::/64 eui-64
latiffesa(config-if)#no shut
```

Figure 31: IPv6 address configured on a router

```
latiffesa(config-if)#do show ipv6 int fa0/0
FastEthernet0/0 is up, line protocol is down
  IPv6 is enabled, link-local address is FE80::210:11FF:FE2E:4A01 [TEN]
  No Virtual link-local address(es):
  Global unicast address(es):
    2001:1::210:11FF:FE2E:4A01, subnet is 2001:1::/64 [EUI/TEN]
  Joined group address(es):
    FF02::1
    FF02::2
```

Figure 32: Router has joined the Multicast group

3. ANYCAST

It is easier to understand anycast if it is said that it is a type of communication that represents "one to nearest". The anycast address is a communication to a group of interfaces on several hosts, where each host is located at different locations. In such a scenario the host that is located nearest to the source host will respond to the multicast *request for communication*. It is a communication that is sent from one interface of a host with a destination of a group of interfaces on several hosts. The anycast address is really a unicast address that is configured on more than one host. The same IPv6 address is used on multiple hosts without the issue of an IP address conflict. It is an exemption that would otherwise not be possible with IPv4. Figure 33 shows that New York will respond to the multicast request from Baldwinsville since it is located nearer to Baldwinsville compared to Los Angeles.

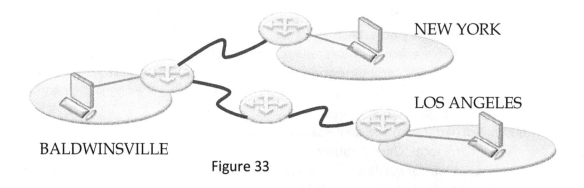

Figure 33

ANYCAST CONFIGURATION EXAMPLE

Server 0 2345::9/64
G'way: 2001:44::4

PC01
IPv6:2001:55::6/64
G'way: 2001:55::5
R0
Fa0/0: 2001:55::5/64

R1
Fa0/0: 2001:44::4/64
2345::/64 anycast
S0/0/1: 2001:10::3/64

Fa0/0

R1

S0/0/1

S0/0/1

R4
S0/0/1: 2001:10::2/64
S0/0/0: 2001:11::2/64
S0/1/1: 2001:66::2/64

R0
S0/1/0

R4

Fa0/0

S0/1/0

S0/0/0

S0/0/0

Server 1 2345::9/64
G'way: 2001:33::3

R2
Fa0/0: 2001:33::3/64
2345::/64 anycast
S0/0/1: 2001:11::3/64

Fa0/0

R2

R1
interface FastEthernet0/0
 ipv6 address 2001:44::4/64
 ipv6 address 2345::/64
anycast
 ipv6 ospf 1 area 0
interface Serial0/0/1
 no ip address
 ipv6 address 2001:10::3/64
 ipv6 ospf 1 area 0
ipv6 unicast-routing
ipv6 router ospf 1
 router-id 1.1.1.1

R2
interface FastEthernet0/0
 ipv6 address 2001:33::3/64
 ipv6 address 2345::/64
anycast
 ipv6 ospf 1 area 0
interface Serial0/0/0
 no ip address
 ipv6 address 2001:11::3/64
 ipv6 ospf 1 area 0
ipv6 unicast-routing
ipv6 router ospf 1
 router-id 2.2.2.2

R4
interface Serial0/0/0
 no ip address
 ipv6 address 2001:11::2/64
 ipv6 ospf 1 area 0
 clock rate 56000
interface Serial0/0/1
 no ip address
 ipv6 address 2001:10::2/64
 ipv6 ospf 1 area 0
 clock rate 56000
interface Serial0/1/0
 no ip address
 ipv6 address 2001:66::2/64
 ipv6 ospf 1 area 0
 clock rate 56000
ipv6 unicast-routing
ipv6 router ospf 1
 router-id 1.0.0.1

R0
interface FastEthernet0/0
ipv6 address 2001:55::5/64
 ipv6 ospf 1 area 0
interface Serial0/1/0
 no ip address
 ipv6 address 2001:66::6/64
 ipv6 ospf 1 area 0
ipv6 unicast-routing
ipv6 router ospf 1
 router-id 3.3.3.3

Server0
IPv6: 2345::9/64
Gateway: 2001:44::4

Server1
IPv6: 2345::9/64
Gateway: 2001:33::3

```
PC>tracert 2345::9

Tracing route to 2345::9 over a maximum of 30 hops:

  1    16 ms     4 ms      6 ms      2001:55::5
  2     5 ms     7 ms      6 ms      2001:66::2
  3    14 ms    12 ms     10 ms      2001:11::3
  4    13 ms    18 ms     21 ms      2345::9

Trace complete.

PC>tracert 2345::9

Tracing route to 2345::9 over a maximum of 30 hops:

  1     2 ms     5 ms      2 ms      2001:55::5
  2     7 ms     7 ms      6 ms      2001:66::2
  3    12 ms    12 ms     15 ms      2001:10::3
  4    20 ms    11 ms     18 ms      2345::9
```

Figure 34

Figure 34 shows how IPv6 address 2345::9 was configured as anycast. The *"ipv6 address 2345::/64 anycast"* command was used on both router R1 and router R2. Also notice that both hosts (Server0 and Server1) are configured with the same IPv6 address of 2345::9/64. The server that is located closest to a requesting host will respond to the communication request for destination IPv6 address for 2345::9/64.

An unicast address can be unicast or activated to be used as anycast. There is no difference in terms of binary or hex value as seen in Figure 35. The unicast address is activated to be anycast only when a supporting anycast device, such as an IPv6 router, is configured with an IPv6 address along with the proper configuration as shown in figure 34.

IPv6 ANYCAST ADDRESS															
← Most significant bit (MSB)								Least significant bit (LSB) →							
1	2	3	4	5	6	7	8	9	10	11	12	13	14	15	16
8 bit	8 bit	8 bit	8 bit	8 bit	8 bit	8 bit	8 bit	8 bit	8 bit	8 bit	8 bit	8 bit	8 bit	8 bit	8 bit
23	45	00	00	00	00	00	00	00	00	00	00	00	00	00	09
2345		0000		0000		0000		0000		0000		0000		0009	
/8	/16	/24	/32	/40	/48	/56	/64	/72	/80	/88	/96	/104	/112	/120	/128

Figure 35: An anycast address is no different than unicast

Unicast communication will help to reduce a lot of wasted Internet bandwidth with a proper placement of *servers* when configured to support anycast address at strategic locations around the world. Routers communicate via multicast communication to share routing and path information among routers that is configured to use the same routing protocols, such as OSPF. The purpose of such information sharing is to make use of the best path to a destination hosts. Anycast communication is a new wave communication methodology that will gradually phase in on most internet routers Based on Figure 34, we can say that anycast refers to the communication whereby the destination is the nearest host interface from a group of hosts that is configured with the same IPv6 address.

The *tracert* command was used on PC01 to analyze the path it takes to a destination host of 2345::9. Based on observation, PC01 will divert its path to host 2349::9 via *network* 2001:10::3 if the original path to address 2349::9 via network 2001:11:3 is purposely disabled using the interface shutdown command.

The address format of IPv6 anycast address when compared to unicast is certainly no different. The IPv6 anycast address is only activated once a system *engineer* configures it to work on participating routers. The following is the command to activate anycast on participating routers.

ipv6 address 2002:0db8:6301::/128 anycast

4. SPECIAL ADDRESSES
There are a few addresses in IPv6 that are categorized as special address:
a. Unspecified
b. Compatibility
    i.   IPv4 Mapped IPv6
    ii.   IPv6 compatible IPv6
c. Loopback
d. Temporary

4a. UNSPECIFIED " :: " .
An unspecified address refers to a host that is not configured with any IPv6 address. This would happen when a host was configured to obtain an IP address from a DHCP6 server but failed to obtain one. During bootup the host will advertise its MAC address along with its "unspecified" address waiting to connect to a DHCP6 server. At this time, the host is using its IPv6 address of "::" (0:0:0:0:0:0:0:0). Refer to Figure 36 of frame 104. A network sniffer application namely Wireshark was used here to show the existence of such transmission that is using a source address of " :: ". The destination address of ff02::1 means that the host is trying to obtain the link layer address of other host that is located in the same network.

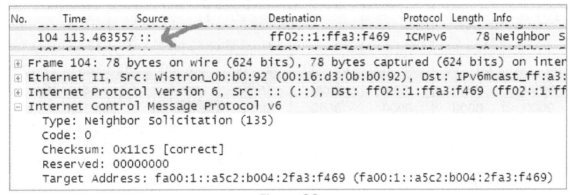

Figure 36

4b. COMPATIBILITY
The purpose of a special compatibility address is to ensure that both IPv4 address and IPv6 address usage is compatible with one another. The two methodologies that were introduced for the purpose of implementation are as follows:

i.   **IPV4-MAPPED IPV6**: The purpose is to allow IPv4 devices that do not support IPv6 to communicate with IPv6 devices. Such addresses begin with eighty zero bits and follow by sixteen bit one. Refer to Figure 37. Such host is categorized as "non IPv6 capable". An example of such address is :
    0:0:0:0:0:ffff:192.168.22.22
    ::ffff:192.168.22.22/96

IPv4 MAPPED IPv6															
1	2	3	4	5	6	7	8	9	10	11	12	13	14	15	16
8 bit	8 bit	8 bit	8 bit	8 bit	8 bit	8 bit	8 bit	8 bit	8 bit	8 bit	8 bit	8 bit	8 bit	8 bit	8 bit
00	00	00	00	00	00	00	00	00	00	11	11	192	168	22	22
0000		0000		0000		0000		0000		1111		C0	A8	16	16
0000		0000		0000		0000		0000		FFFF		192.168.22.22			
										::FFFF :192 .168 .22 .22					
/8	/16	/24	/32	/40	/48	/56	/64	/72	/80	/88	/96	/104	/112	/120	/128

Figure 37: Example of an address used for a "non IPv6 capable" host

ii. IPV4-COMPATIBLE IPv6 ::/96

IPv4 is used by devices that are categorized as "IPv6 aware". In this case, the IPv6 compatible address has 0 for all the 96 *high-order* bits followed by the IPv4 address for the lower order 32 bits. The format of IPv4-compatible IPv6 *address* is **0:0:0:0:0:0:A.B.C.D** or ::A.B.C.D where A,B,C and D represent an IPv4 address in hex. The entire 128 bit sequence is the host IPv6 address. Refer to the methodology to convert decimal to hex in the upcoming chapter.

IPv4-COMPATIBLE IPv6															
1	2	3	4	5	6	7	8	9	10	11	12	13	14	15	16
8 bit	8 bit	8 bit	8 bit	8 bit	8 bit	8 bit	8 bit	8 bit	8 bit	8 bit	8 bit	8 bit	8 bit	8 bit	8 bit
00	00	00	00	00	00	00	00	00	00	00	00	192	168	22	22
0000		0000		0000		0000		0000		0000		C0	A8	16	16
0000		0000		0000		0000		0000		0000		192.168.22.22			
										::c0a8 :1616 or ::192.168.22.22					
/8	/16	/24	/32	/40	/48	/56	/64	/72	/80	/88	/96	/104	/112	/120	/128

Figure 38: Example of an address used for an "IPv6 aware" host

Devices that require communication with both IPv4 and IPv6 hosts will make use of IPv4-compatible IPv6 addresses to communicate with IPv4 only hosts and IPv6 only hosts. The following figure shows the conversion process of the thirteen and fifteen octet from decimal to hexadecimal:

1. Convert from decimal to binary
2. Separate the eight groups bit into parts of four bits
3. Convert all the four binary bits to hexadecimal.

IPv4	192.168.22.22
IPv6	0000:0000:0000:0000:0000:0000:c0a8:1616
SUMMARIZED	0:0:0:0:0:0:c0a8:1616
COMPRESSED	::c0a8:1616

Figure 39a: Conversion of an IPv4 address to IPv6

IPv4 COMPATIBLE IPv6															
13								14							
1	2	3	4	5	6	7	8	1	2	3	4	5	6	7	8
192								168							
11000000								10101000							
1100				0000				1010				1000			
8	4	2	1	8	4	2	1	8	4	2	1	8	4	2	1
1	1	0	0	0	0	0	0	1	0	1	0	1	0	0	0
C				0				A				8			

Figure 39b: detail of the 13th and 14th octets

IPv4 compatible IPv6 will allow the use of *tunneling* to allow IPv6 hosts to communicate with other hosts in a network that still uses IPv4 address format.

4c. LOOPBACK "::1" .

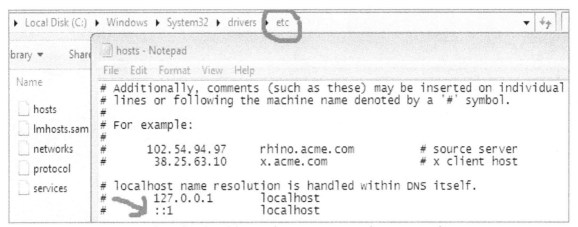

Figure 40: loopback address shown in a Windows Host directory

This address is similar to the loopback (localhost) address of IPv4 of 127.0.0.1. For IPv6 the address of "::1" has been allocated for loopback purposes. It is used by hosts for inter process communication. The difference between IPv4 loopback and IPv6 loopback is IPv4 loopback has allocated one <u>block</u> of addresses as loopback where as IPv6 has allocated only one <u>address</u>. All operating systems have a file named "hosts" in their directory. This file contains the loopback address that is used by the operating system. For Microsoft operating systems the host file is in the C:\windows\system32\drivers\etc directory whereas Linux and Unix will be in the /etc directory.

4d. TEMPORARY ADDRESSES

Every computer or modem that connects to the Internet is allocated a public IPv4 address. Every time the line is disconnected and reconnected again there is that possibility that the same IPv4 address will be allocated again. The IP address allocation is given by a server that manages the IP address allocation. This server is known as DHCP server. This type of public IPv4 IP address allocation not only limits the Internet application usage but it also imposes a privacy concern due to the fact that the Internet session might be monitored by a third party unknowingly.

Figure 41 shows where you can check the allocation of the Public IP address for IPv4 or IPv6 on internet connected devices. The top figure shows that if a PC is connected directly to the internet using a modem (without a router or wireless access point), then the public IP address allocated to the user by the ISP (internet Service Provider) can be identified by checking the configuration on the PC itself.

The bottom of Figure 41 shows that if the user has an access point/router between the user and the modem, then the Public IP address allocated can be identified by checking the configuration on the access point. This is always the case where the modem is configured in "bridge" mode.

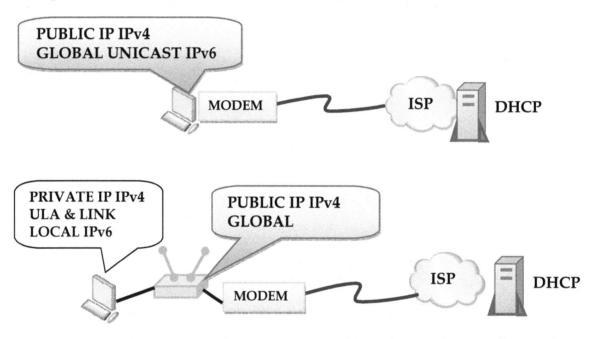

Figure 41: Check the configuration on the PC (top) or at the access point (bottom).

IPv6 prefix allocation is given by a router through router advertisements known as stateless address auto configuration. If the interface ID is using the format EUI-64 (mac address) format, the user's Internet activity and usage could be easily monitored. This is because the MAC address of each host, be it a computer, switch or router is unique. *This has become a privacy concern to Internet users*. This issue has been debated and the resolution is to make use of temporary addresses in IPv6. The Interface ID portion will be generated at random and will change from time to time based on the user's activity. This is known as random interface identifier. More information on this is available in RFC 3041. Once a preset lifetime expires, a new interface ID will be generated for the temporary address of IPv6. The current setup can be determined by using the *"netsh int ipv6 show privacy"* command, or it can be enabled with the *"netsh int ipv6 set privacy state=enable"* command.

```
C:\>netsh int ipv6 show privacy
Querying active state...
Temporary Address Parameters
Use Temporary Addresses        : enabled
Duplicate Address Detection Attempts: 5
Maximum Valid Lifetime         : 7d
Maximum Preferred Lifetime          : 1d
Regenerate Time                     : 5s
Maximum Random Time                 : 10m
```

Figure 42: Use the *show privacy* command to determine the current setup

4e. DOCUMENTATION ADDRESSES

The documentation in RFC 3849 has assigned the 2001:db8::/32 address prefix for the use of IPv6 related documentation. The address prefix can be used for training purposes and for any reason such as network simulation related to the IPv6 protocol. This address prefix is not allowed to be routed through the public internet.

Reference
https://tools.ietf.org/html/rfc3587
http://tools.ietf.org/html/rfc4291?referring_site=bodynav
https://tools.ietf.org/html/rfc4193
https://tools.ietf.org/html/rfc4193
http://www.iana.org/assignments/ipv6-multicast-addresses/ipv6-multicast-addresses.xhtml
https://tools.ietf.org/html/rfc3306
https://tools.ietf.org/html/rfc5952
http://www.ietf.org/rfc/rfc2373.txt
https://www.ietf.org/rfc/rfc3484.txt

Chapter 5
ADDRESS SCOPE
AND HEXADECIMAL

- Introduction to Hexadecimal
- MAC address
- The Address scope of IPv6

INTRODUCTION TO HEXADECIMAL

Hexadecimal is a base 16 numbering system. It is different when compared to binary which is base two and base ten for decimal. Hexadecimal is also known as hex. The base 16 numbering system of hexadecimal begins from zero to nine and continues from A to F, that is: 0123456789ABCDEF. Each hex value is the same as four binary. Each hex digit is also one *nibble*.

	→															
HEXADECIMAL	0	1	2	3	4	5	6	7	8	9	A	B	C	D	E	F
DECIMAL	0	1	2	3	4	5	6	7	8	9	10	11	12	13	14	15

ADDING HEX

The following example shows how to add the hex value of 7 and 6 which gives a total of D.

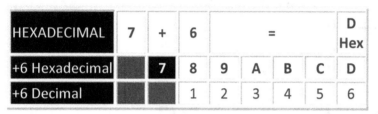

HEXADECIMAL	7	+	6		=		D Hex
+6 Hexadecimal		7	8	9	A	B	C	D
+6 Decimal			1	2	3	4	5	6

Adding Hexadecimal D+4=11

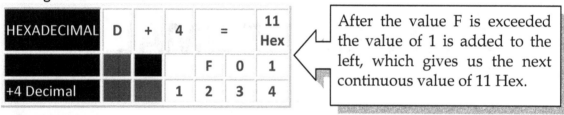

HEXADECIMAL	D	+	4		=		11 Hex
				F	0	1
+4 Decimal			1	2	3	4

After the value F is exceeded the value of 1 is added to the left, which gives us the next continuous value of 11 Hex.

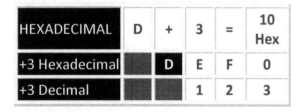

HEXADECIMAL	D	+	3	=	10 Hex
+3 Hexadecimal		D	E	F	0
+3 Decimal			1	2	3

The above example shows how the value of hex D is being added with 4 to give a total of 11 hex. The four value after D is E, F, 0 than 1. Because the added total supersede the value of F, the value of 1 needs to be added on the left . Another example is, if the hex value of D is added to 3 it will give us a total of 10 hex.

Figure 43 is an example on how to convert a decimal 580 to hex; Figure 44 shows how to convert 256.

CONVERT DECIMAL 580 TO HEX				
EXPLANATION	CALCULATION	ANSWER	REMAINDER	HEX
1. Divide 580 by 16 = 36.25. 2. .25x16 =4	580/16	36	4	
1. Divide 36 by 16 = 2.25. 2. .25x16=4	36/16	2	4	↑
1. Because the value of 2 is lower than 16, so we stop the calculation here.	2/16	-	2	244
Decimal 580 is equal to hex 244				

Figure 43

CONVERT DECIMAL 256 TO HEX		
CALCULATION	ANSWER	REMAINDER
256/16	16	0
16/16	1	0
1/16	-	1
HEX :		100

Figure 44

MAC ADDRESSES

The Acronym *MAC* comes from the word Media Access Control. Media means the transmission medium used such as wire to transmit signals. The meaning of "Access Control" is the set of rules to comply on order to media. Lastly, *address* refers to the address value in hexadecimal.

Figure 45: MAC address of this host is F0-DE-F1-D5-6C-41

The MAC address is used interchangeably with "physical address", "adapter address", "IEEE 802 address" and "burn-in address". Figure 45 shows the Physical Address that is used by the current host. The MAC address of a host can be determined with the following steps.

1. Start | Search | ncpa.cpl
2. Local Area Connection | Status | Details.

A MAC address value is in the format of hexadecimal. Every manufacturer of layer two devices and layer three devices of the OSI Model will require the allocation of MAC addresses. The allocation is managed by the Institute of Electrical and Electronic Engineer (IEEE) that is based in the United States. A MAC address consists of 48 bits and is allocated to each network interface card. An IP address is binded to the operating system where a MAC address is binded to the hardware. A MAC address is a fixed value (burn-in Address-BIA) to the hardware. It can be written in the format of F0-DE-F3-D5-66-41 or F0:DE:F3:D5:66:41.

The first three octets, the first twenty four bits, refer to the manufacturer of the network interface card (Figure 46). The subsequent three octets that follow is a random value that is determined by the manufacturer. Every manufacturer is allocated a specific code that is known as the Organizational Unit Identifier (OUI). A large scale manufacturer would be allocated several OUI values.

MAC ADDRESS (48 bit)					
OUI			NIC		
24 bit			24 bit		
Octet 1	Octet 2	Octet 3	Octet 4	Octet 5	Octet 6
F0	DE	F1	D5	6C	41
1111 0000	1101 1110	1111 0001	1101 0101	0110 1100	0100 0001
F0-DE-F1			D5-6C-41		
F0-DE-F1-D5-6C-41					

Figure 46: Breakdown of a MAC address

The manufacturer of the network interface card can be identified by using its OUI at http://standards.ieee.org/develop/regauth/oui/public.html as shown below. This OUI is identified by the manufacturer name of "Wistron".

Search the Public OUI/'company_id' Listing
Search for: F0-DE-F1   Search!   clear field

MAC addresses allow hosts to communicate with each other at the data link layer of the OSI Model. It allows hosts to communicate before a logical address is configured or allocated to the host. Logical address is also known as an IP address. MAC address is the hardware part of the communication whereas an IP address is the application or operating system part of the communication. MAC address is permanent with the hosts whereas IP address may change when at different locations. Figure 47 summarizes this concept very well:

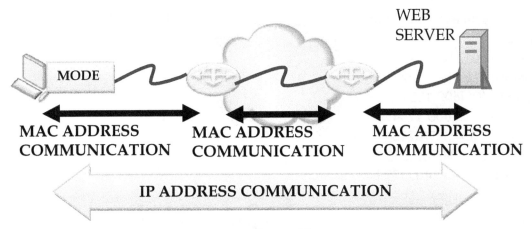

Figure 47

The way of communication today is via "IP networks". Every host in an IP network will record the mapping of IP address to MAC address in a cache memory. This cache memory is known as Address Resolution Protocol (ARP) cache. Other communication such as DHCP depends on the MAC address to record the IP address allocation given to DHCP hosts. The *arp-a* command allows us to view the arp cache. The same such communication is still maintained in IPv6 but with a slightly different approach. It is known as Network Discovery protocol (NDP). A detail explanation on NDP will be explained in a later chapter. Figure 48 shows the arp cache of a host.

```
C:\>arp -a
Interface: 192.168.2.209 --- 0xc
  Internet Address        Physical Address      Type
  192.168.2.200           1c-7e-e5-aa-41-85     dynamic
  192.168.2.204           00-13-02-d1-33-70     dynamic
  192.168.2.210           00-13-02-d1-33-70     dynamic
  192.168.2.255           ff-ff-ff-ff-ff-ff     static
  224.0.0.22              01-00-5e-00-00-16     static
  224.0.0.252             01-00-5e-00-00-fc     static
  239.255.255.250         01-00-5e-7f-ff-fa     static
  255.255.255.255         ff-ff-ff-ff-ff-ff     static
```

Figure 48: arp cache of a host

THE ADDRESS SCOPE OF IPv6

Figure 49 indicates the value of IPv6 address which starts from 0000:0000:0000:0000:0000:000:0000:0000 to ffff:ffff:ffff:ffff:ffff:ffff:ffff:ffff, in the format of hexadecimal.

BIT	16	16	16	16	16	16	16	16
FIRST IP ADDRESS	0000	0000	0000	0000	0000	0000	0000	0000
LAST IP ADDRESS	ffff	ffff	ffff	ffff	ffff	ffff	ffff	ffff

Figure 49

The following is an example of the address scope for IPv6 prefix FD00:1234:5678:2154/64.

Prefix/L: FD

Global ID : 0012345678

Subnet ID: 2154

Combine/CID: fd00:1234:5678:2154::/64

IPv6 addresses: fd00:1234:5678:2154::/64:XXXX:XXXX:XXXX:XXXX

Start: fd00:1234:5678:2154:0000:00000:00000:00000

End : fd00:1234:5678:2154:ffff:ffff:ffff:ffff

Total host: 18446744073709551616

NET ID	ADDRESS SCOPE FD00:0004:0018:0054::/64			
	FIRST IP	SCOPE		LAST IP
FD00:18:54:0::/64	FD00:18:54:0:0:0:0:0	0:0:0:1	ffff:ffff:ffff:fffe	FD00:18:54:0:ffff:ffff:ffff:ffff
FD00:18:54:1::/64	FD00:18:54:1:0:0:0:0	0:0:0:1	ffff:ffff:ffff:fffe	FD00:18:54:1:ffff:ffff:ffff:ffff
FD00:18:54:2::/64	FD00:18:54:2:0:0:0:0	0:0:0:1	ffff:ffff:ffff:fffe	FD00:18:54:2:ffff:ffff:ffff:ffff
FD00:18:54:3::/64	FD00:18:54:3:0:0:0:0	0:0:0:1	ffff:ffff:ffff:fffe	FD00:18:54:3:ffff:ffff:ffff:ffff
FD00:18:54:4::/64	FD00:18:54:4:0:0:0:0	0:0:0:1	ffff:ffff:ffff:fffe	FD00:18:54:4:ffff:ffff:ffff:ffff
FD00:18:54:5::/64	FD00:18:54:5:0:0:0:0	0:0:0:1	ffff:ffff:ffff:fffe	FD00:18:54:5:ffff:ffff:ffff:ffff

NOTE:

1. IPv6 do not have addresses that are categorized as **"NETWORK ADDRESS"** or **"BROADCAST ADDRESS"**. All IPv6 addresses can be used.
2. There is a total of 18446744073709551616 IP addresses for each /64 network.

Figure 50: Address scope for prefix FD00:1234:5678:2154/6

Reference

https://tools.ietf.org/html/rfc2464

https://tools.ietf.org/html/rfc3513

https://tools.ietf.org/html/rfc4007

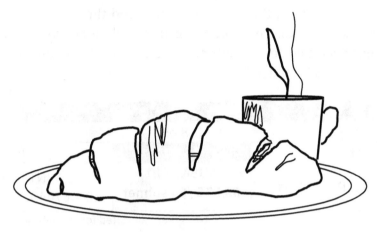

Chapter 6
SUBNETTING

- Introduction to Subnetting
- Subnetting Method 1: Binary Calculation
- Subnetting Method 2 : Table Lookup
- Subnetting Method 3: Nibble
- Point to Point Connections
- Subnet Router Anycast Address

INTRODUCTION TO SUBNETTING

Subnetting in IPv6 serves the same purpose as in IPv4. Both will make use of binary 1 to define the mask value. Some differences when compared between IPv4 and IPv6 are:

a. The mask format: IPv6 uses the hex format.

b. The bits that are allocated for the mask purpose: from the 49th bit to the 63rd bit.

In IPv4, part of the IP address is the network portion and the part that follows represent the host. The same applies to IPv6. The only thing that is different in IPv6 is a portion of IPv6 address is allocated specifically for subnetting; that is, from the 49 bit to the 64 bit, which is a total of 16 bits (see Figures 51 and 52).

IPv6		
128 bit		
48 bit	16 bit	64 bit
GLOBAL ROUTING PREFIX	SUBNET ID 65,536 /64 subnet	INTERFACE ID 18446744073709551616 host

Figure 51: The 49th to the 64th bit are allocated for subnetting

1	2	3	4	5	6	7	8	9	10	11	12	13	14	15	16
8 bit	8 bit	8 bit	8 bit	8 bit	8 bit	8 bit	8 bit	8 bit	8 bit	8 bit	8 bit	8 bit	8 bit	8 bit	8 bit
20	01	0d	b8	85	a3	00	42	10	00	8a	2e	03	70	73	34
2001		0db8		85a3		0042		1000		8a2e		0370		7334	
/8	/16	/24	/32	/40	/48	/56	/64	/72	/80	/88	/96	/104	/112	/120	/128
REGISTRY /23															
ISP PREFIX /32															
SITE PREFIX /48															
SUBNET PREFIX /64															

Figure 52: The first 48 bits determine routing over the Internet; the next 16 are for subnetting.

Straight-forward simple subnetting

If a block *address* of 2637:f238/32 is allocated to an Internet Service Provider (ISP), the ISP then can allocate one of the following prefix to its customers.

2637 : f238 /32	Allocated to ISP
16bit: 16bit /32	Binary
2637 : f238 : XXXX /48	Allocation to customers is /48
16bit: 16bit: 16bit /48	Binary

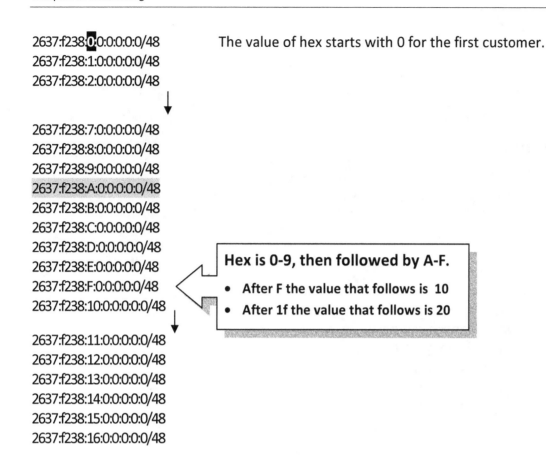

2637:f238:0:0:0:0:0:0/48
2637:f238:1:0:0:0:0:0/48
2637:f238:2:0:0:0:0:0/48

↓

2637:f238:7:0:0:0:0:0/48
2637:f238:8:0:0:0:0:0/48
2637:f238:9:0:0:0:0:0/48
2637:f238:A:0:0:0:0:0/48
2637:f238:B:0:0:0:0:0/48
2637:f238:C:0:0:0:0:0/48
2637:f238:D:0:0:0:0:0/48
2637:f238:E:0:0:0:0:0/48
2637:f238:F:0:0:0:0:0/48
2637:f238:10:0:0:0:0:0/48

↓

2637:f238:11:0:0:0:0:0/48
2637:f238:12:0:0:0:0:0/48
2637:f238:13:0:0:0:0:0/48
2637:f238:14:0:0:0:0:0/48
2637:f238:15:0:0:0:0:0/48
2637:f238:16:0:0:0:0:0/48

The value of hex starts with 0 for the first customer.

Hex is 0-9, then followed by A-F.

- After F the value that follows is 10
- After 1f the value that follows is 20

The conclusion is the prefix allocation will be as follows:

- Allocation to is ISP: /32
- Allocation to organization is: /48
- Allocation to each subnet (vlan) in an organization is : /64

An allocation for an organization is 2637:f238:A:0:0:0:0:0/48. The organization needs to be segmented into 6 vlan. A total of 6 subnets are required. They are:

VLAN 1: 2637:f238:A:0:0:0:0:0/64
VLAN 2: 2637:f238:A:1:0:0:0:0/64
VLAN 3: 2637:f238:A:2:0:0:0:0/64
VLAN 4: 2637:f238:A:3:0:0:0:0/64
VLAN 5: 2637:f238:A:4:0:0:0:0/64
VLAN 6: 2637:f238:A:5:0:0:0:0/64

↓

2637:f238:A:C:0:0:0:0/64
2637:f238:A:D:0:0:0:0/64
2637:f238:A:E:0:0:0:0/64
2637:f238:A:F:0:0:0:0/64
2637:f238:A:10:0:0:0:0/64

WAN
<S0/0>
2637:f238:A:0:0:0:0:1/64

   | |
   | |
2637:f238:A:0:0:0:0:2/64
 <S0/0>
ROUTER01
 <Fa0/0>=== ===SWITCH L3====
VLAN 1:2637:f238:A:1:0:0:0:1/64

FIRST IP   LAST IP
| |==VLAN2 2637:f238:A:2:0:0:0:2/64- ffff:ffff:ffff:ffff
| |==VLAN3 2637:f238:A:3:0:0:0:2/64- ffff:ffff:ffff:ffff
| |==VLAN4 2637:f238:A:4:0:0:0:2/64- ffff:ffff:ffff:ffff
| |==VLAN5 2637:f238:A:5:0:0:0:2/64- ffff:ffff:ffff:ffff
| |==VLAN6 2637:f238:A:6:0:0:0:2/64- ffff:ffff:ffff:ffff
| |==VLAN7 2637:f238:A:7:0:0:0:2/64- ffff:ffff:ffff:ffff

LAYER 3 SWITCH IP ADDRESS
INT VLAN 1 2637:f238:A:1:0:0:0:2/64
INT VLAN 2 2637:f238:A:2:0:0:0:1/64
INT VLAN 3 2637:f238:A:3:0:0:0:1/64
INT VLAN 4 2637:f238:A:4:0:0:0:1/64
INT VLAN 5 2637:f238:A:5:0:0:0:1/64
INT VLAN 6 2637:f238:A:6:0:0:0:1/64
INT VLAN 7 2637:f238:A:7:0:0:0:1/64

NET ID	IPv6 ADDRESS SCOPE			
	FIRST IP	**RANGE IP**		**LAST IP**
2637:f238:A:0::/64	**2637:f238:A:0**:0:0:0:0	0:0:0:1	ffff:ffff:ffff:fffe	2637:f238:A:0:ffff:ffff:ffff:ffff
2637:f238:A:1::/64	**2637:f238:A:1**:0:0:0:0	0:0:0:1	ffff:ffff:ffff:fffe	2637:f238:A:1:ffff:ffff:ffff:ffff
2637:f238:A:2::/64	**2637:f238:A:2**:0:0:0:0	0:0:0:1	ffff:ffff:ffff:fffe	2637:f238:A:2:ffff:ffff:ffff:ffff
2637:f238:A:3::/64	**2637:f238:A:3**:0:0:0:0	0:0:0:1	ffff:ffff:ffff:fffe	2637:f238:A:3:ffff:ffff:ffff:ffff
2637:f238:A:4::/64	**2637:f238:A:4**:0:0:0:0	0:0:0:1	ffff:ffff:ffff:fffe	2637:f238:A:4:ffff:ffff:ffff:ffff
2637:f238:A:5::/64	**2637:f238:A:5**:0:0:0:0	0:0:0:1	ffff:ffff:ffff:fffe	2637:f238:A:5:ffff:ffff:ffff:ffff

Figure 53: Scope of 6 subnets in above example

SUBNETTING METHOD 1: Binary Calculation

This method is best learned through a couple of example problems:

Example Question 1: You are responsible to implement an IPv6 network in your organization. Your organization is allocated a global address prefix of 3FFA:FF2B:4D:B000::/51. All the hosts in each of your four vlan need to be allocated an IP address and subnet mask. What is the prefix for the fourth vlan?

A. 3FFA:FF2B:4D:C800::/53?   B. 3FFA:FF2B:4D:B400::/53?

C. 3FFA:FF2B:4D:C000::/53?   Or   D. 3FFA:FF2B:4D:F000::/55?

F	B000	hexadecimal value of the subnet ID being subnetted
N	4	Number of subnet required
S	2	Number of bits required for subnetting
M	51	The original prefix value
48	/48	site prefix
16	Base 16	hexadecimal

Figure 54: Data for Question 1

Solution for Question 1:

First calculate the number of bits, f, that need to be allocated (fixed):

$f = M - 48$, or $51 - 48 = 3$

Next, calculate, i, the incremental value of subnet:

$i = 2^{[16-(f+S)]}$

$i = 2^{[16 - (3+2)]}$

$2^{11} = 2048$

Then, convert 2048 to hexadecimal:

CONVERT DECIMAL TO HEX				
EXPLANATION	CALCULATION	ANSWER	REMAINDER	HEX
Divide the original value by 16	2048/16	128	0	
Divide the "answer" by 16	128/16	8	0	↑
Divide the balance by 16	8/16	0	8	
				800
Decimal 2048 is equivalent to hex 0800				

Next, calculate each subnet:

1. First Subnet (F) = B000
2. Second Subnet = B000 + 800 = B800
3. Third Subnet = B800 + 800 = C000
4. Fourth Subnet = C000 + 800 = C800

HEXADECIMAL	B	8	0	0		1.	8 + 8 (9,A,B,C,D,E,F,**0**)
HEXADECIMAL		8	0	0		2.	Once the value of F has been exceeded add one to B, changing the value of B to C.
TOTAL	C	0	0	0		3.	B800 + 800 = C000

Figure 55: Adding 800 to B800 in Hexadecimal

Finally, calculate the prefix value, using the formula of M+S:
/51+2 = /53

Thus, the prefixes for each subnet are:
First Subnet: 3FFA:FF2B:4D:B000/53
Second Subnet: 3FFA:FF2B:4D:B800/53
Third Subnet: 3FFA:FF2B:4D:C000/53
Forth Subnet: 3FFA:FF2B:4D:C800/53 (Answer is "A")

Example Question 2: As a network support engineer you are responsible for overseeing the migration process from IPv4 to IPv6. Your organization has been allocated global address prefix of **2001:2222:3333:4400::/54**. The hosts for each of the existing four vlans needs to be allocated an IP address and prefix. Is the prefix for the third vlan(subnet)...

A. 2001:2222:3333:4400::/58?
B. 2001:2222:3333:4440::/58?
C. 2001:2222:3333:4480::/58? Or
D. 2001:2222:3333:44C0::/58?

F	4400	hexadecimal value of the subnet ID being subnted
N	12	Number of subnet required
S	4	Number of bit required for subnetting 2^x = >12
M	54	The original prefix value
48	/48	site prefix
16	Base 16	hexadecimal

Figure 56: Data for Question 2

Solution for Question 2:

f = M – 48, or 54 - 48 = 6

i = 2^[16-(f+S)]

i = 2^[16 – (6+4)];

2^ 6 = 64

Converting to hexadecimal:

CONVERT DECIMAL TO HEX				
EXPLANATION	CALCULATE	ANSWER	ACCESS	HEX
Divide by 16.	64/16	4	**0**	↑ **40**
Divide Access by 16. If the access value is less than 16 the answer will be 0.	4/16	0	**4**	
Decimal 64 is equal to hex 40				

Each subnet is calculated:

First Subnet ,F = **4400**

Second Subnet = 4400 + 40 = **4440**

Third Subnet   = 4440 + 40 = **4480**

Fourth Subnet = 4480 + 40 = **44C0**

HEXADECIMAL	4	4	8	0		1.	8 + 4 (9,A,B,**C**)
HEXADECIMAL			4	0		2.	After 9, the value of 10 equals A.
TOTAL	4	4	C	0		3.	4480 + 40 = 44C0

Figure 57: adding 40 to 4480 in hexadecimal

The prefix value is calculated:

/51+4 = /58

First Subnet: 2001:2222:3333:4400::/58

Second Subnet: 2001:2222:3333:4440::/58

Third Subnet: 2001:2222:3333:4480::/58   Answer is "C"

Fourth Subnet: 2001:2222:3333:44C0::/58

Figure 58 on the next page shows the address scope for each of these subnets.

NET ID ::/58	IPv6 ADDRESS SCOPE				
	First IP	RANGE		LAST IP	
2001:2222:3333:4400	2001:2222:3333:4400: 0:0:0:0	0:0:0:1	ffff:ffff:ffff:fffe	22001:2222:3333:4400: ffff:ffff:ffff:ffff	
2001:2222:3333:4440	2001:2222:3333:4440: 0:0:0:0	0:0:0:1	ffff:ffff:ffff:fffe	2001:2222:3333:4440: :ffff:ffff:ffff:ffff	
2001:2222:3333:4480	2001:2222:3333:4480: 0:0:0:0	0:0:0:1	ffff:ffff:ffff:fffe	2001:2222:3333:4480: ffff:ffff:ffff:ffff	
2001:2222:3333:44C0	2001:2222:3333:44C0: 0:0:0:0	0:0:0:1	ffff:ffff:ffff:fffe	2001:2222:3333:44C0: ffff:ffff:ffff:ffff	

Figure 58: Address Scope for 4 subnets calculated in Question 2

SUBNETTING METHOD 2: Table Lookup

Like Method 1, this method is best learned with an example problem.

Example Question 3: Your organization has been allocated an IPv6 address of 2001:db8:cc12:aa00::/56 by the ISP. You are given the task to allocate IPv6 addresses to three site offices. Identify the three subnets required.

Solution for Question 3:

Using Table A and B, follow Steps 1-4 below:

TABLE A																			
1	2	3	4		5	6	7	8		9	10	11	12		13	14	15	16
2	0	0	1	:	0	d	b	8	:	c	c	1	2	:	a	a	0	0
1 to 4	5 to 8	9 to 12	13 to 16		17 to 20	21 to 24	25 to 28	29 to 32		33 to 36	37 to 40	41 to 44	45 to 48		49 to 52	53 to 56	57 to 60	61 to 64

IPv6 value from column 1 to 14 should be maintained as in step number 3

Figure 59 (Table A): Most Significant Bit Lookup Table with 2001:db8:cc12:aa00 entered in top row.

TABLE B			
SUBNET REQUIRED	THE VALUE OF X	+	SEQUENCE
2	1	8	0 , 8
4	2	4	0 , 4 , 8 , C
8	3	2	0 , 2 , 4 , 6 , 8 , A , C , E
16	4	1	0 , 1 , 2 ,3 , 4 , 5 , 6 , 7 , 8 , 9 , A , B , C , D , E , F

Figure 60 (Table B): Increment Number Lookup Table

Step 1:
Identify the number of bits (x) required:
1. $2^x = 3$ subnet
2. X = 2 (from Table B). The value of x is two, because 2^2 is equal to 4, and four is the nearest value to fulfill the requirement of three subnets.
3. /56 + 2 = /58
4. This means all the three subnets will use prefix **/58**

Step 2:
Identify the additional "+" required.
5. Refer to table B
6. If the "**number of subnet required**" is 4, the value of X is 2 the calculations should be an increment of 4 (+4)
7. The sequence is identified as 0 , 4 , 8 , C

Step 3:
Identify the value of MSB (Most Significant Bit) that is required.
8. In step 1 we already identified the required prefix as /58. Referring to table A, the IPv6 address value from column 1 to 14 must be fixed, which is the value highlighted: **2001:db8:cc12:aa**00::/58. The 15th bit will designate the subnets: 2001:db8:cc12:aa**0**0::/58.

Step 4:
Just simply add the sequence identified in step 2 to the first 14 fixed bits as follows:

- Subnet 1: 2001:db8:cc12:aa**0**0::/58
- Subnet 2: 2001:db8:cc12:aa**4**0::/58
- Subnet 3: 2001:db8:cc12:aa**8**0::/58
- Subnet 4: 2001:db8:cc12:aa**C**0::/58 (not used, as only 3 subnets are desired).

If we choose to do so, the same method of calculation can be used to further divide our step 4 result from /58 to /60 as needed by the organization. This is shown in the hierarchical figure below:

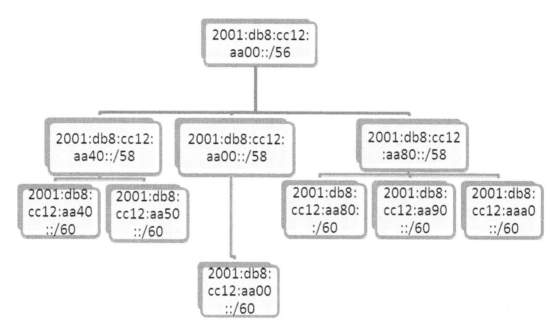

Figure 61: The IPv6 Address of 2001:db8:cc12:aa00::/56 broken down further into /58 and /60 subnets

SUBNETTING METHOD 3: NIBBLE SUBNETTING

The huge number of bits available in IPv6 makes you worry or wonder how subnetting should be done. When allocated a /48 subnet there could be many possibilities of making mistakes. The following guidelines will help to avoid such mistakes

- Every 4 bits is a nibble and each nibble is one character in the IPv6 address.
- Each set in the IPv6 address is 16 bits.
- There is no need to be concerned about address wastage. A Prefix of /64 can be used for a point to point connection with /128 as the loopback.

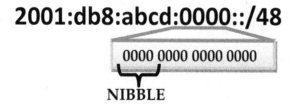

Figure 62: A nibble is 4 bits; each set, or *octet*, is 16 bits

There are two factors that are very important when designing or restructuring a network. These two factors are summarization and hierarchical. Summarization will reduce the size of the routing table taking less memory on the routers, whereas hierarchical allows faster connectivity from one network to the other. The following example will use the IPv6 address of 2001:db8:abcd:0000:/48 where 0000 will be used for the purpose of subnet calculation.

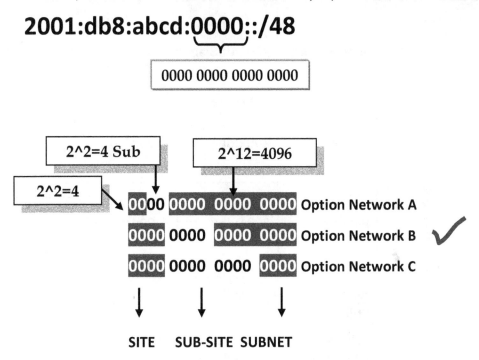

Figure 63: Example of Nibble Subnetting

Referring to Figure 63, there are many possible subnetting options – three are shown. In this example we will choose Option B, where the first 4 bits are chosen for the site, the second 4 for the subsite and the last 8 for the subnet. This will produce 16 (2^4) sites, 16 (2^4) subsites, and 256 (2^8) subnets. The topology layout for Network B is shown below:

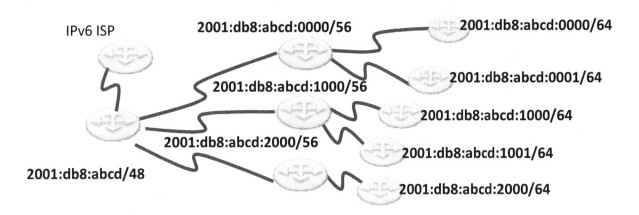

Figure 63a: Nibble Network Infrastructure

2001:db8:abcd:0000 ::/48			
	STATE :/52	CITY :/56	VLAN :/64
1	2001:db8:abcd:X	2001:db8:abcd:0X	2001:db8:abcd:00XX
1.1	SELANGOR 2001:db8:abcd:0000::/52	Shah Alam — 2001:db8:abcd:0000::/56	Firewall:0000::/64 DMZ: 0001::/64 VLAN 1 :0002::/64 VLAN 2: 0003::/64 VLAN 3: 0004::/64
1.2		Petaling Jaya — 2001:db8:abcd:0100::/56	Firewall:0100::/64 DMZ: 0101::/64 VLAN 1 :0102::/64 VLAN 2: 0103::/64
1.3		Banting — 2001:db8:abcd:0200::/56	Firewall:0200::/64 DMZ: 0201::/64 VLAN 1 :0202::/64 VLAN 2: 0203::/64
1.4		Kelang — 2001:db8:abcd:0300::/56	
1.5		Jelutung — 2001:db8:abcd:0400::/56	↓
1.6		Ttdi — 2001:db8:abcd:0500::/56	
1.7		Subang — 2001:db8:abcd:0600::/56	
1.8		Subang Jaya — 2001:db8:abcd:0700::/56	
1.9		Glenmarie — 2001:db8:abcd:0800::/56	
1.10		Damansara — 2001:db8:abcd:0900::/56	
1.16		LAST CITY — 2001:db8:abcd:0F00::/56	Firewall:0F00::/64 (LAST): 0FFF::/64
NOTE: ALWAYS ENSURE THAT THERE IS AVAILABLE RESERVE SUBNET IN CASE THE NEED ARISE ONCE THE ORGANIZATION EXPANDS.			
2	2001:db8:abcd:X	2001:db8:abcd:1X	2001:db8:abcd:1XXX
2.1	KUALA LUMPUR 2001:db8:abcd:1000::/52	Cheras — 2001:db8:abcd:1000::/56	Firewall:1000::/64 DMZ: 1001::/64 VLAN 1 :1002::/64
2.2		Bkt Bintang — 2001:db8:abcd:1100::/56	↓
2.3		Kpg Pandan — 2001:db8:abcd:1200::/56	
2.4		Selayang — 2001:db8:abcd:1300::/56	
2.16		LAST CITY — 2001:db8:abcd:1F00::/56	Firewall:1000::/64 (LAST): 1FFF::/64

Figure 63b

- In figure 63b more detail is shown. Every branch office in each state is connected to several site offices. The plan using "Network B" will allow us to get 16 states (sites), 16 Cities (subsites) and 256 subnets.

Figure 64 above, shows another example. Here we have a large organization name LAT with branch offices in every state in the USA. LAT wants to upgrade the existing IPv4 network to an IPv6 network. Every branch office is responsible to over look the operations of several site offices that reports to them regularly. A decision has been made to go for "Option Network C" (from Figure 63) that can support 16 states (sites), 256 cities (subsites) and 16 site offices.

	STATE :/52	CITY :/60		VLAN :/64
		2001:db8:1234:0000 ::/48		
1	2001:db8:1234:X	2001:db8:1234:00X		2001:db8:1234:000X
1.1		City A	2001:db8:1234:	Firewall:
				DMZ:
				VLAN 1 :
				VLAN 2:
				VLAN 3:
1.2		City B	2001:db8:1234:	Firewall:
				DMZ:
				VLAN 1 :
				VLAN 2:
1.3	NEW YORK 2001:db8:1234:0000::/52	City C	2001:db8:1234:	Firewall:
				DMZ:
				VLAN 1 :0022::/64
				VLAN 2: 0023::/64
1.4		City D	2001:db8:1234:	
1.5		City E	2001:db8:1234:	
1.6		City F	2001:db8:1234:	
1.7		City G	2001:db8:1234:	
1.8		City H	2001:db8:1234:	
1.9		City I	2001:db8:1234:	
1.10		City J	2001:db8:1234:	
1.16		LAST CITY	2001:db8:abcd:	Firewall:
				(LAST):
NOTE: ALWAYS PLAN FOR A RESERVE SUBNET IN CASE THE NEED ARISE.				
2	2001:db8:1234:X	2001:db8:1234:00X		2001:db8:1234:000X
2.1		City K	2001:db8:abcd:1234::/60	Firewall:1000::/64
	CALIFORNIA 2001:db8:1234:1000::/52			DMZ: 1001::/64
				VLAN 1 :1002::/64
2.2		City L	2001:db8:1234:	
2.3		City M	2001:db8:1234:	
2.4		City N	2001:db8:1234:	
2.16		LAST CITY	2001:db8:1234:	Firewall:1000::/64
				(LAST): 1FFF::/64

Figure 64

IPv6 POINT TO POINT (P2P) /64, /126, /127, /128

A point to point connection which is mostly used over a WAN link will only require two IP addresses. The discussion of using IPv6 over point to point connection has been one of the most debated. Details on the matter, RFC's along with its solutions and concerns are listed below.

	RFC	PREFIX /127 AND /64 ISSUES
1	3627	• **"Use of /127 Prefix Length Between Routers Considered Harmful".** This is due to any anycast communication issue related to "subnet router anycast address". • STATUS: Historic. • Obsoleted by: RFC 6164
2	5375	• The usage of the /127 addresses, the equivalent of IPv4's RFC 3021, is not valid and should be strongly discouraged. • STATUS: Informational. • Additionally the documentation on **"IPV6 UNICAST ADDRESS ASSIGNMENT CONSIDERATIONS,"** states that: Using /64 subnets is strongly recommended, also for links connecting only routers". A deployment compliant with the current IPv6 specifications cannot use other prefix lengths."
3	ARIN	• Documentation on **"IPV6 ADDRESSING PLANS"** clearly states that: • "No subnets will use prefixes longer than /64**."** • "IETF expects that you will assign a /64 for point-to-point links".
Note: All the information here discourages the /127 prefix for point to point.		

		PREFIX /126 FOR POINT TO POINT
1		• Configuring IPv6 address based on EUI-64 on a router point to point connection is not practical. • This approach is similar to using /30 in IPv4 days.

	RFC	PREFIX /64 POINT TO POINT ISSUES
1	2463	• If an IPv6 host receives a packet destination for a network that is the same as its interface, though the destination is not for its interface, the packet must be forwarded to the same subnet. • PIING PONG ATTACK: If a substantial amount of packet with the same destination network as the P2P is injected into link and it is known that the destination addresses is not reachable the packet will bounce back and forth between both interfaces

		causing congestion. Further detail explanation at the end of this chapter. • STATUS: Draft Standard • Obsoleted by: RFC 4443

	RFC	ADVANTAGE OF PREFIX /127 over P2P
1	2463	• RFC 2463 will resolve this problem. Routers MUST support the assignment of /127 prefixes on point-to-point inter-router links. Routers MUST disable Subnet-Router anycast for the prefix when /127 prefixes are used.
2	6164	• Neighbor Cache Exhaustion Issue: "The use of a 64-bit prefix length on an inter-router link that uses Neighbor Discovery (e.g., Ethernet) potentially allows for denial-of-service attacks on the routers on the link". The use of /127 allows for two address only eliminating such possibility. • STATUS: Informational
NOTE: SOLUTION FOR N0. 2 RFC 6164: Only a point to point ethernet link would require NDP. The solution to this issue is to disable NDP over ethernet point to point. RFC 6164 conflicts with RFC 5375.		

	RFC	SOLUTION FOR ISSUES IN RFC 2463 AND 6164
1	4443	• If an IPv6 hosts receives a packet with a destination network the same as that of the receiving interface, though its destination address is not for the same as that of the receiving interface in actuality, the packet should be discarded. This document obsolete RFC 2463 • STATUS: Draft Standard

Before discussing best practices for P2P, further explanation of two of the issues above are warranted

A. RFC 3627: "/127 PREFIX IS DOCUMENTED AS HARMFUL"

The following explains what is meant by "Use of /127 Prefix Length between Routers Considered Harmful".

1. Two routers, A and B, are connected as point to point.
2. A is configured with 2001:db8:1234:5678::1/127 and later on B is configured with 2001:db8:1234:5678::0/127.
3. Once A is configured with the IPv6 address it sends out DAD and it passes the test.
4. A adds the subnet anycast address which is 2001:db8:1234:5678::0/127. DAD is now disabled because anycast address can reside on more than one interface.
5. B is now configured with 2001:db8:1234:5678::0/127. Once B activates DAD it will fail.

B. RFC 2463 and RFC 4443: "PING PONG ATTACK"

In RFC 2463 which was made obsolete by 4443, a ping-pong attack is an exploit on ICMPv6. The issue is explained here.

1. Two routers, A and B, are connected as point to point.
2. A is configured with 2001:db8:1234:5678::1/64 and later B is configured with 2001:db8:1234:5678::2/64.
3. A receives a packet with a destination address of 2001:db8:1234:5678::3/64. This is the subnet address for both router point to point links. This is not A's interface address.
4. A will forward the packet into the subnet of 2001:db8:1234:5678::/64 which is its interface with an address of 2001:db8:1234:5678::1/64. This packet will arrive at B.
5. B receives a packet with a destination address of 2001:db8:1234:5678::3/64. This is the subnet address for both router point to point links. This is not B's interface address.
6. B will forward the packet into the subnet of 2001:db8:1234:5678::/64 which is its interface with an address of 2001:db8:1234:5678::2/64. This packet will arrive at A. The process repeats itself all over again.

Best Practice for Point to Point Links

(Refer to Figure 65a to 65c below.) There are many ways of configuring your point to point links. It does however depend on your ISP and the RFC that the hardware supports. You may encounter some hardware that does not support /127, this simply means you don't have the option but to use /126 or /64. The following is the recommended guideline for point-to-point implementations:

a. Allocate prefix /64 for the point to point link. Then configure the prefix /127 on both point to point links. Should there be an issue using the /127 in the future, change the /127 back to /64. This consideration would be useful in a small organization.
b. Allocate prefix /64 for the point to point link, then use prefix /64 to make the point to point connection. This configuration would be suitable in either a small or large organization.
c. Point-to-point links may be assigned a /126 prefix if there is written assurance that the issue documented in RFC 3627 will not occur.

Choosing a setup option would depend on the following factors, which can be used as a checklist:
1. You need to match what your ISP setup, that is
   a. What are their current practise and policies?
   b. What does their existing hardware support?
   c. What is their plan for future hardware support?
2. You need to work with whatever RFC your IPv6 hardware supports.
3. You will need to allocate a prefix /64 to your point to point links.
4. Lastly with all the above in mind you have three options that is:
   a. Continue with /64
   b. Choose to use /127. (EUI-64 not supported)
   c. Choose to use /126.(EUI-64 not supported)

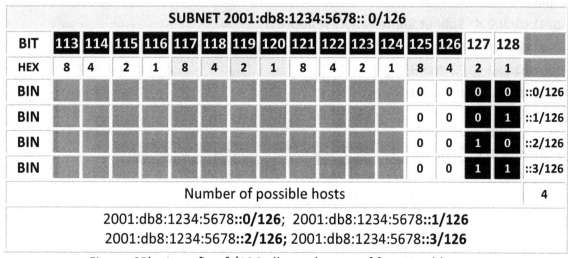

Figure 65a: A prefix of /127 allows the use of two IP addresses

Figure 65b: A prefix of /126 allows the use of four IP addresses

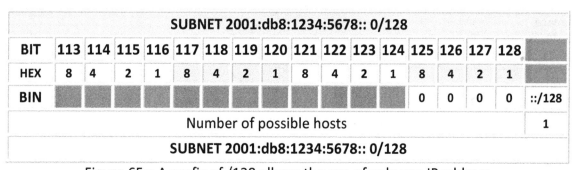

Figure 65c: A prefix of /128 allows the use of only one IP address

SUBNET ROUTER ANYCAST ADDRESS

An anycast address is also a unicast address and both cannot be distinguished from one another. A subnet-router anycast address would be a better example of an anycast address. Assume a host was assigned with the following global IPv6 address:

Host address: 2001:0db8:1234:5678:220:33ff:4433:7766/64

The subnet-router anycast address is actually the least significant 64 bits, which is the suffix. The all zero address in each subnet is known as "all router anycast address".

Subnet-router anycast address: 2001:0db8:1234:5678::/64

Example 1: **2001:db8::/64**

> **2001:db8::0 <- Subnet Router-anycast address**
>
> **2001:db8::1 <-** Router A
>
> **2001:db8::2 <-** Router B
>
> **2001:db8::3 to 2001:db8::ffff:ffff:ffff:ffff <-** not used

Example 2: **2001:db8::/126**

> **2001:db8::0 <- Subnet Router-anycast address**
>
> **2001:db8::1 <-** Router A
>
> **2001:db8::2 <-** Router B
>
> **2001:db8::3 <-** not used

Example 3: **2001:db8::/127**

> **2001:db8::0 <- Router A conflicts with Subnet Router-anycast address**
>
> **2001:db8::1 <-** Router B

Note: There aren't enough addresses to support anycast communication in example 3.

Reference

https://tools.ietf.org/html/rfc5942
https://tools.ietf.org/html/rfc5375
https://tools.ietf.org/html/rfc6177
http://techxcellence.net/2011/05/09/v6-subnetting-made-easy/
https://www.ietf.org/rfc/rfc2526.txt
https://tools.ietf.org/html/rfc6164
https://www.ietf.org/rfc/rfc2463.txt
https://www.ietf.org/rfc/rfc4443.txt
https://www.ietf.org/rfc/rfc5375.txt
https://www.ietf.org/rfc/rfc3627.txt
https://tools.ietf.org/html/rfc6177

Chapter 7
ROUTE
SUMMARIZATION

SUMMARIZATION IPv6

Route summarization is also known as **aggregation** and **supernetting**. Summarization reduces the size of the routing table so that the router can process the route faster with less resources. Route *summarization* in IPv6 is the same as IPv4, except:

- IPv6 is 128 bit where as IPv4 is 32 bit
- IPv6 is in hex whereas IPv4 in decimal

It is best explained through a number of examples:

Example 1: *Summarize* the IPv6 addresses below:

- FEC0:0:0:A:125:23FF:FEE2:1F53
- FEC0:0:0:E:10A:9FFF:FED7:D3

1. Part of the addresses are similar (highlighted):
   FEC0:0:0:000A:125:23FF:FEE2:1F53
   FEC0:0:0:000E:10A:9FFF:FED7:D3

2. Convert the value to binary.
   FEC0:0000:0000: 0000 0000 0000 1010: = A
   FEC0:0000:0000: 0000 0000 0000 1110: = E

3. Identify up to the point of similarity.

   | 16 | 16 | 16 | 4 | 4 | 4 | 1 | = 61 = /61 |

   FEC0:0000:0000: 0000 0000 0000 1010: = A
   FEC0:0000:0000: 0000 0000 0000 1110: = E

4. Add 0 bit where there is no similarity
   FEC0:0000:0000: 0000 0000 0000 1000:

5. Convert from binary to hex
   FEC0:0000:0000: 0000 0000 0000 1000:
   FEC0: 0 : 0 : 8   ::/61
       Answer: FEC0:0:0:8::/61

Example 2: Summarize the following IPv6 address to reduce the processing overhead on the routers.
   2001:CC1E:2AB3:1A3C::/64
   2001:CC1E:2AB3:1A4D::/64

We will use the same method as how we would work with IPv4 summarization. Compare the portion of both addresses up to the point where the values are not the same. The similarity ends at 1A which is in the fourth group of 4 hexadecimal digits.
1A3C
1A4D

a. Convert both values from hex to binary.

Hex   Binary

1A3C: 0001 1010 0011 1100

1A4D: 0001 1010 0100 1101

b. Similarity is up to the **9**th bit

1A3C: 0001 1010 0011 1100

1A4D: 0001 1010 0100 1101

c. Change the bits after to 0.

1A3C: 0001 1010 0000 0000

1A4D: 0001 1010 0000 0000

d. Convert from binary to hex

1A3C: 0001 1010 0000 0000

1A4D: 0001 1010 0000 0000

       1   **A**   **0**   **0**

e. Insert the 1A00 value in its original place. .

2001:CC1E:2AB3:1A3C::/64

2001:CC1E:2AB3:1A4D::/64

2001:CC1E:2AB3:1A00::/64

f. Count the new prefix value:

2001:CC1E:2AB3:1A3C::/64

2001:CC1E:2AB3:1A4D::/64

   16 + 16 + 16 + 9   **::/57**

g. The summarization is **2001:CC1E:2AB3:1A00::/57**

The following is another example of IPv6 route summarization. An IPv6 address of 2001:DB8:acc:4/64 is a summarization of the following four addresses:

- 2001:DB8:acc:**4**::/64

- 2001:DB8:acc:**5**::/64

- 2001:DB8:acc:**6**::/64

- 2001:DB8:acc:**7**::/64

The similarity bit are the most significant bit of "01" for the binary value of four, five, six and seven that is:

- 0100

- 0101

- 0110

- 0111

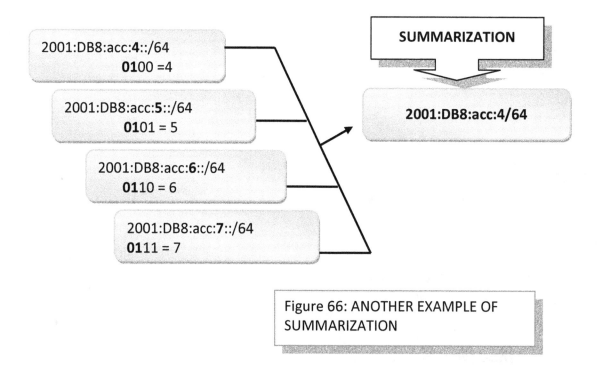

Figure 66: ANOTHER EXAMPLE OF SUMMARIZATION

Reference
https://tools.ietf.org/html/rfc1887
http://www.cisco.com/c/en/us/td/docs/ios-xml/ios/ipv6/configuration/xe-3s/ipv6-xe-36s-book/ip6-stat-routes.html
https://ccie20728.wordpress.com/2008/06/26/ipv6-summarization/

Chapter 8
EUI-64

INTRODUCTION TO EUI-64

EUI is an acronym for Extended Unique Identifier. It is a numbering system standard managed by IEEE. The IEEE is an organization that is responsible for the allocation of MAC addresses that consists of 48 bits in hexadecimal. The MAC address format is based on EUI-48.

Figure 67 illustrates the methodology of using EUI-64 to allocate IPv6 addresses to hosts in different subnets. EUI-64 allows the allocation of addresses without the need for manual configuration. This method makes use of the MAC address *"interface Ethernet"* to restructure the combination based on the EUI-64 specification. The conversion process is explained in the next section.

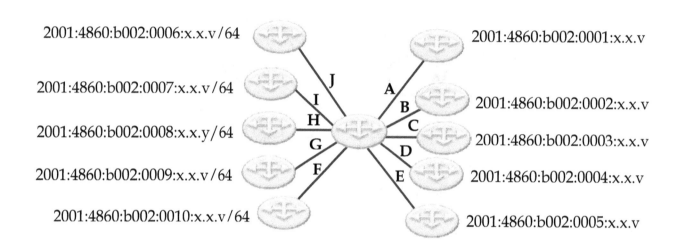

Serial A	2001:4860:b002:0001: w.x.y.z	2001:4860:b002:0001: w.x.y.z
Serial B	2001:4860:b002:0002: w.x.y.z	2001:4860:b002:0002: w.x.y.z
Serial C	2001:4860:b002:0003: w.x.y.z	2001:4860:b002:0003: w.x.y.z
Serial D	2001:4860:b002:0004: w.x.y.z	2001:4860:b002:0004: w.x.y.z
Serial E	2001:4860:b002:0005: w.x.y.z	2001:4860:b002:0005: w.x.y.z
Serial F	2001:4860:b002:0006: w.x.y.z	2001:4860:b002:0006: w.x.y.z
Serial G	2001:4860:b002:0007: w.x.y.z	2001:4860:b002:0007: w.x.y.z
Serial H	2001:4860:b002:0008: w.x.y.z	2001:4860:b002:0008: w.x.y.z
Serial I	2001:4860:b002:0009: w.x.y.z	2001:4860:b002:0009: w.x.y.z
Serial J	2001:4860:b002:0010: w.x.y.z	2001:4860:b002:0010: w.x.y.z

Figure 67

EUI-64 CONVERSION

First Step:

Convert the 48 bit MAC address to 64 bit. First, the MAC address needs to be separated into two parts whereby each part is 24 bits. The first part will be the OUI and the other part is the value unique to the NIC. Every network interface card manufacturer will be allocated an OUI which is the first 24 bits of the MAC address. After that a value of **0xFFFE** will be inserted between the OUI and the last 24 bits. Refer to Figure 68a.

58: 94:6B: 32:F0:60

58: 94:6B   32:F0:60

58: 94:6B: FFFE 32:F0:60

Figure 68a

The above example is known as EUI-48 that translates to EUI-64 with an FFFE. There is another version of EUI-64 that doesn't use MAC address, and is known as "Real EUI-64".

Second Step:

Change the 7th bit of the OUI. An IPv6 address that will be used locally will allocate bit 1 for the 7th bit. If it is global, then the 7th bit will be bit 0. The resulting address is known as **modified EUI-64.** The following example, Figure 68b, shows how the FE80::5A:94:6B:FFFE 32:F0:60 address was generated.

58: 94:6B: FFFE 32:F0:60

5 8: 94:6B: FFFE 32:F0:60

0101 1000: 94:6B: FFFE 32:F0:60

0101 1010: 94:6B: FFFE 32:F0:60

0101 1010: 94:6B: FFFE 32:F0:60

5   A: 94:6B: FFFE 32:F0:60

5A:94:6B: FFFE 32:F0:60

FE80::5A:94:6B: FFFE 32:F0:60

Figure 68b

To verify the modified EUI-64 value we configure it on a device router. Figure 69a and 69b are the output of the interface on the Cisco router model 1941.

```
latiffesa(config)#do show interface FastEthernet0/0
FastEthernet0/0 is administratively down, line protocol is down (disabled
   Hardware is Lance, address is 5894.6b32.f060 (bia 0030.f2b4.6701)
```

Figure 69a

```
Latiffesa(config)#int fa0/0
Latiffesa(config-if)#ipv6 address 2001::/64 eui-64
Latiffesa(config-if)#do sho ipv6 int bri
FastEthernet0/0            [administratively down/down]
    FE80::5A94:6BFF:FE32:F060
    2001::5A94:6BFF:FE32:F060
FastEthernet0/1            [administratively down/down]
Vlan1                      [administratively down/down]
```

Figure 69b

THE 7th LEAST SIGNIFICANT BIT

The 7th bit is known as Universal/Local bit, also U/L. That particular bit refers to interface configuration whether it is local or global. Bit 0 refers to global while bit 1 refers to local. The U/L is a preset value by the IEEE. The purpose for this differentiation is to support current technology without sacrificing the future needs of the new technology. IPv6 continues to evolve and change now and then as documented in the RFC 4291. Figure 70 shows the 7th LSB in more detail for MAC address F0-DE-F1-D5-6C-41 and prefix 2001:db8:8543:0042::/64.

1	2	3	4	5	6	7	8	9	10	11	12	13	14	15	16
8 bit	8 bit	8 bit	8 bit	8 bit	8 bit	8 bit	8 bit	8 bit	8 bit	8 bit	8 bit	8 bit	8 bit	8 bit	8 bit
20	01	0d	b8	85	a3	00	42	F0	DE	F1	FF	FE	D5	6C	41
2001		0db8		85a3		0042		F0DE		F1FF		FED5		6C41	
/8	/16	/24	/32	/40	/48	/56	/64	/72	/80	/88	/96	/104	/112	/120	/128

9								10							
1	2	3	4	5	6	7	8	1	2	3	4	5	6	7	8
F				0				D				E			
8	4	2	1	8	4	2	1	8	4	2	1	8	4	2	1
1	1	1	1	0	0	0	0	1	1	0	1	1	1	1	0
F				0				D				E			
				Change bit 0 to bit 1											
				0	0	1	0								
F				2				D				E			

Figure 70: The 7th LSB

2001:db8:85a3:42:f2de:f1ff:fed5:6c41

Reference
https://tools.ietf.org/html/rfc4291
http://packetlife.net/blog/2008/aug/4/eui-64-ipv6/
https://www.ietf.org/rfc/rfc3572.txt

Chapter 9
ICMPv6

- THE PURPOSE OF ICMPv6
- ERROR & INFORMATION MESSAGES
- DHCPv6 & ICMPv6
- TYPE AND CODE ICMPv6

THE PURPOSE OF ICMPv6

ICMPv6 is the latest version of the ICM (Internet Control Message) protocol. It plays an important role to fulfill the many requirements to complete successful communication using Internet Protocol version 6. ICMPv6 itself consists of multiple functions that are identifiable by code and type. Since the first version of ICM protocol, its purpose has been "error reporting". The ICMP is required to gather information regarding the status of the communication path. Other than that, it also allows hosts to gather information about other hosts that are within the same scope of network. This leads to faster and efficient communication between communicating hosts. Figure 71 illustrates the ICMPv6 header. The protocol number 58 has been allocated for the ICMPv6 protocol. The ICMP protocol serves two main purposes:

- Error Messages
- Information Messages

ICMPv6 HEADER (58)			
00 01 02 03 04 05 06 07	08 09 10 11 12 13 14 15	16 17 18 19 20 21 22 23	24 25 26 27 28 29 30 31
TYPE (8 bit)	CODE (8 bit)	CHCKSUM (16 bit)	
ICMPv6 message : The bit size is based on the type and code that is utilised			

Figure 71

ERROR AND INFORMATION MESSAGES

**Error Messages** are categorized under "Type" 1 to 127. ICMPv6 error messages are divided further into four main categories:

a. **Destination Unreachable**. It is a type of error message from a gateway that dictates a network that is not reachable.

b. **Time Exceeded**. It is a message from the gateway about a TTL value that has reached the value of 0. The packet will be discarded. TTL is short for Time To Live. It is a value allocated to a packet as a preset time period that dictates the length of time that the packet can stay active on the wire.

c. **Packet Too Big.** Each and every operating system and network equipment has a preset maximum value that dictates the maximum size packet that it is capable to handle, called the MTU(Maximum Transmission Unit). This message contains information that maximum size (MTU) allowable along the path has been exceeded.

d. **Parameter Problems**. This message dictates that a field in the IPv6 extension header was not recognized and will not be processed.

**Information Messages** are categorized under "Type" 128 and thereafter. Information messages can be categorised into three main categories.

a. **Diagnostic Messages**. The ping command uses ICMPv6 for Echo Request and Echo Reply. The ping command is useful to identify network connectivity issues. Echo request message is sent by the source host whereas echo reply is the reply message from the destination host. .

b. **Neighbor Discovery Messages**. NDP is the acronym for Neighbor Discovery Messages. It is introduced to replace the ARP communication in IPv4. The Neighbor discovery protocol is used for the following reasons:

- To obtain the data-link (MAC address) address of other hosts that is in the same network via multicast.
- To identify active hosts in the current network.
- To identify hosts that functions as routers.

There are five categories of NDP messages to assist the process of neighbor discovery. They are:

- Type 133: Router Solicitation
- Type 134: Router Advertisement
- Type 135: Neighbor Solicitation
- Type 136: Neighbor Advertisement
- Type 137: Redirect

Refer to Figure 72 below for more detail.

IPV6 ICMPv6 NEIGHBOR DISCOVERY (ND) MESSAGE	
ROUTER SOLICITATION	RA is a request for the local router to send a multicast router advertisement. Router advertisement contains the information that is required by the host to communicate in the existing network. It contains the network prefix.
ROUTER ADVERTISEMENT (RA)	The local router will send RA into the network at a specified interval. It is also produced by a router in respond to a router solicitation message.
NEIGHBOR SOLICITATION	This is a request that all host in the network to send information about its link layer.
NEIGHBOR ADVERTISEMENT	This is in response to a Neighbor Solicitation Message.
REDIRECT	It is a message from other router to all hosts that a better route exists to a required destination.

Figure 72: Types of ICMPv6 ND Messages

c. **Multicast Group Management.** The multicast communications that is referred to here is Multicast Listener Discovery (MLD). There are three categories.

- Multicast Listener Query. A multicast from a router for the purpose of identifying other hosts that is in the same group of multicast listener.

- Multicast Listener Report. Host that receives the multicast listener query from the router will reply with a multicast listener report if the host chose to receive the multicast traffic from the same category.

- Multicast Listener Done. Any host that no longer wants to receive multicast will send a Multicast Listener Done as a method of informing its intention to leave the multicast group.

ICMPv6 and DHCPv6

There are two methods to implement DHCPv6, they are:

a. **Stateless:** The word *stateless* means a session that will not be entirely monitored from start to end. A router will allocate a network prefix without the need to record or monitor any session thereafter. The router will not allocate any DNS configuration to network hosts. If the hosts in the network require DNS IP configuration this will need to be obtained from a DHCPv6 which can be activated on a Microsoft Windows Server 2012.

b. **Stateful:** *Stateful* means a situation where the entire communication session is monitored from the first point of contact right to the time when the session is terminated. A Microsoft Windows Server 2012 acting as a DHCPv6 will document all the IP address allocated by requesting hosts. The entire IP configuration can be obtained from the DHCPv6 server, even without a router if the network administrator wishes to do so. This situation happens when no router sends out router advertisements (RA) or a situation where a router requires that a host obtains its DNS configuration from a DHCPv6. This is normally the way to go when security is the main concern.

The following discussion will further explain the workings of the <u>stateless</u> setup while the stateful setup will be explained in its own chapter (Chapter 11) entitled *DHCPv6*. The workings of the stateful setup is best being supported by the DHCPv6 server service running on Microsoft Windows Server 2012.

The diagram below shows the many options to choose from in order to setup the IPv6 address configuration on host computers. Each option has its pros and cons. The uniqueness of each network indicates that the best option depends on the existing network infrastructure and current organization policies.

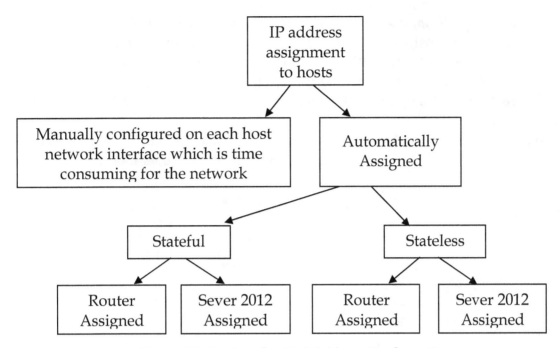

Figure 73: Options for IPv6 Address Configuration

It is safe to say that the stateful option would best fit in most common and general type network infrastructure that's being used widely today though future technologies might have a different approach.

Stateless configuration requires one or both of the following setup:

1. An IPv6 router to allocate the *network prefix*
2. Optionally, a DHCPv6 *server* to allocate other IP configuration where required.

PC01: Windows 7/8

  1. BEFORE:

IPv6: ::
MAC: 00:16:d3:0b:b0:92

  2. AFTER:

IPv6: FA00:1::a5c2:b004:2fa3:f469
GATEWAY: FE80::225:84ff:fef4:1b69

```
latiffesa >enable
latiffesa #conf t
latiffesa(config)#ipv6 unicast-routing
latiffesa(config)#interface fastethernet 0/0
latiffesa(config-if)#ipv6 address fa00:1::/64
eui-64
latiffesa(config-if)#ipv6 enable
latiffesa(config-if)#no shut
latiffesa(config-if)#end
```

Figure 74a

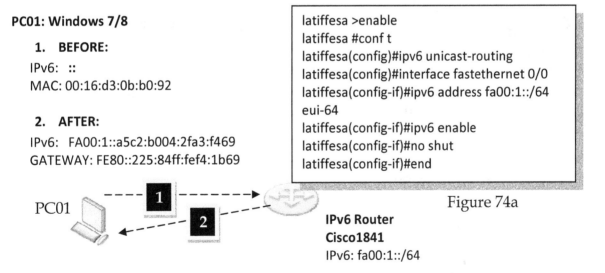

PC01

IPv6 Router
Cisco1841
IPv6: fa00:1::/64

When an IPv6 host *boots up*, it will send a *message* known as network *discovery* (ND) into the network. A router in that network will respond to the network discovery message by allocating a network prefix to the hosts via multicast. The host that receives the network prefix will then combine it with its interface ID (mac address or random ID) to make up a complete IPv6 address. Figure 74a is an example of such implementation.

Figure 74c, on the next page, details the process of obtaining the address from the router in Figure 74a. Figure 74b, below, shows successful execution of these operations.

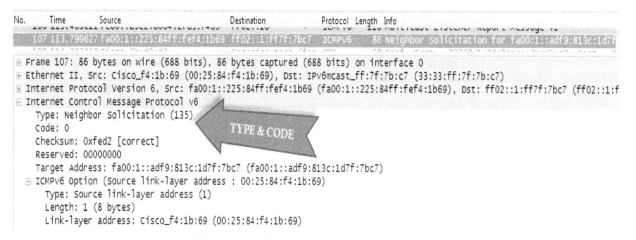

Figure 74b: ICMPv6-Neighbor Solicitation

NO	EXPLANATION	COMMUNICATION
1	PC01 will start by generating its own Link Local Address from its MAC address or *randomly*. It will than send a Duplicate Address Detection (DAD) as in the next step which is step 2 .	Localhost

2	Source IP: ::
	 Destination IP: ff02::1:ffa3:f469
	 Source MAC: 00:16:d3:0b:b0:92
	 Destination MAC: 33:33:ff:a3:f4:69
	 ⊞ Ethernet II, Src: Wistron_0b:b0:92 (00:16:d3:0b:b0:92), Dst: IPv6mcast_1
	 ⊞ Internet Protocol Version 6, Src: :: (::), Dst: ff02::1:ffa3:f469 (ff02
	 ⊟ Internet Control Message Protocol v6
	    Type: Neighbor Solicitation (135)
	    Code: 0
	    Checksum: 0x0d46 [correct]
	    Reserved: 00000000
	    Target Address: fe80::a5c2:b004:2fa3:f469 (fe80::a5c2:b004:2fa3:f469)
		ICMPv6, Type: 135 Code: 0
		 Neighbor Solicitation from PC01.
		
		 Duplicate Address Detection (DAD)

3	Source IP: fe80::a5c2:b004:2fa3:f469 Destination IP: ff02::2 Source MAC: 00:16:d3:0b:b0:92 Destination MAC: 33:33:00:00:00:02	ICMPv6, Type: 133 Code: 0 **Router Solicitation** from PC01.
4	Source IP: fe80::225:84ff:fef4:1b69	ICMPv6 Type 134 code 0

	Destination IP:ff02::1
	Source MAC: 00:25:84:f4:1b:69
	Destination MAC: 33:33:00:00:00:01)
	<pre>⊟ Flags: 0x00
	    0... .... = Managed address configuration: Not set
	    .0.. .... = Other configuration: Not set
	    ..0. .... = Home Agent: Not set
	    ...0 0... = Prf (Default Router Preference): Medium (0)
	    .... .0.. = Proxy: Not set
	    .... ..0. = Reserved: 0
	Router lifetime (s): 1800
	Reachable time (ms): 0
	Retrans timer (ms): 0
	⊞ ICMPv6 Option (Source link-layer address : 00:25:84:f4:1b:69)
	⊞ ICMPv6 Option (MTU : 1500)
	⊞ ICMPv6 Option (Prefix information : fa00:1::/64)</pre>
		Router Advertisement (RA) from router.

5	PC01 will generate a Global or Site Local Address from the prefix that it receives. It will again send a Duplicate Address Detection (DAD) in step 6.	Localhost

6	PC01 wll now use its global or site local
	<pre>⊞ Ethernet II, Src: Wistron_0b:b0:92 (00:16:d3:0b:b0:92), Dst: IPv6mcast_ff:a:
	⊞ Internet Protocol Version 6, Src: :: (::), Dst: ff02::1:ffa3:f469 (ff02::1:f
	⊟ Internet Control Message Protocol v6
	    Type: Neighbor Solicitation (135)
	    Code: 0
	    Checksum: 0x11c5 [correct]
	    Reserved: 00000000
	    Target Address: fa00:1::a5c2:b004:2fa3:f469 (fa00:1::a5c2:b004:2fa3:f469)</pre>
		ICMPv6, Type: 135 Code: 0
		Neighbor Solicitation from PC01. Duplicate Address Detection (DAD)

7	PC01 will use the routers IP address as its default gateway configuration.	Localhost

Figure 74c: The process of obtaining an IPv6 address from a router

TYPE and CODE

Figure 75 illustrates some of the many categories of ICMPv6 types and codes that are commonly used in computer networks today. Type 135 code 0 is used for neighbor solicitation.

ICMPv6 TYPE & CODE		
TYPE	**COMMUNICATION**	**EXPLANATION**
0	Reserve	-
1	Destination unreachable.	• Code 0: *No route to destination*. • Code 1: *Communication with destination administratively prohibited*. There is the probability that a firewall is blocking the communication. • Code 2: beyond scope of source address. For example the scope of the source address is link local but the destination is global. • Code 3: *Address Unreachable*. An attempt failed to obtain the layer 2. • Code 4: *Port unreachable*. The destination port is not configured to

		• accept the incoming communication.
2	Packet too big.	• Code 0: The packet has exceeded the MTU size.
3	Time exceeded.	• Code 0: *Hop limit exceeded in transit.* • Code 1: *Fragment reassembly time exceeded.*
4	Parameter problem.	• Code 0: Erroneous header field encountered • Code 1 :Unrecognized next header type • Code 2: Unrecognized IPv6 option
128	Echo request.	• Code 0: It is used by the ping command to test connections.
129	Echo reply.	• Code 0: It is a reply to the ping command.
130	**MLD** Group Membership Query. -	• Router or switch will transmit MLD to determine the available hosts that is a multicast listener.
131	**MLD** Group Membership Report.	• When a host receives a multicast listener query, the host that is in the same multicast group will respond by sending its information.
133	**NDP** Router Solicitation. (**RS**)	• Code 0: After boot up a host will send this type of NDP in order to identify the existing router in the network that will send out router advertisement.
134	**NDP** Router Advertisement. (**RA**)	• Code 0: The router sends out RA at fixed interval that contains network configuration information such as network prefix.
135	**NDP** Neighbor Solicitation. (**NS**)	• Code 0: An NS message replaces the ARP. The purpose of this message is to obtain information about other hosts link layer address and at the same time informs other hosts of its local link layer address.
136	**NDP** Neighbor Advertisement. (**NA**)	• Code 0: This message is a response to the NS message. It is a response to the NS message.
137	Redirect.	• Code 0: This message is sent out by a router to inform other hosts that a much better route exists to a specific destination.

Figure 75

ETHERNET II HEADER (minimum size 64 byte)		
0 0 0 0 0 0 0 0 0 0 1 1 1 1 1 1 1 1 1 1 2 2 2 2 2 2 2 2 2 2 3 3 3 3 3 3 3 3 3 3 4 4 4 4 4 4 4 4 0 1 2 3 4 5 6 7 8 9 0 1 2 3 4 5 6 7 8 9 0 1 2 3 4 5 6 7 8 9 0 1 2 3 4 5 6 7 8 9 0 1 2 3 4 5 6 7		
Destination address (48 bit)		
Source address (48 bit)		
Ethertype 0x86dd (16 bit)	Data ::: (46 – 1500 byte)	

IPv6 HEADER (0x86dd) 40 byte		
00 01 02 03 04 05 06 07 08 09 10 11 12 13 14 15 16 17 18 19 20 21 22 23 24 25 26 27 28 29 30 31		
Version	Traffic Class	Flow Label
Payload Length	Next Header = 58	Hop Limit
Source address (128 bit)		
Destination address (128 bit)		
Data atau Extension Header 1 (EH=58) ICMP		

ICMPv6 HEADER (58)		
00 01 02 03 04 05 06 07 08 09 10 11 12 13 14 15 16 17 18 19 20 21 22 23 24 25 26 27 28 29 30 31		
Type 8 bit	Code 8 bit	Checksum 16 bit
ICMPv6 message: the size depends on the type and code.		

Figure 76

Figure 76 illustrates the contents of each field in each protocol while Figure 78a shows the breakdown of each one of them from a packet sniffer point of view, namely Wireshark. Figure 77 shows each protocol identified as a hex value.

NO	ETHER TYPE	PROTOCOL
1	0x800	Internet Protocol Version 4 (IPv4)
2	0x806	Address Resolution Protocol (ARP)
3	0x0842	Wake-On-LAN
4	0x8035	Reverse Address Resolution Protocol (RARP)
5	0x8100	Vlan Tagged Frame 802.1q
6	0x86dd	Internet Protocol Version 6 (IPv6)
7	0x8847	MPLS Multicast
8	0x88cc	Link layer discovery protocol (LLDP)

Figure 77

No.	Time	Source	Destination	Protocol	Length	Info
12	13.2805060	::	ff02::1:ffa3:f469	ICMPv6	78	Neighbor Solicitation for fe

⊞ Frame 12: 78 bytes on wire (624 bits), 78 bytes captured (624 bits) on interface 0
⊟ Ethernet II, Src: Wistron_0b:b0:92 (00:16:d3:0b:b0:92), Dst: IPv6mcast_ff:a3:f4:69 (33:33:ff:a3:f4:69)
  ⊟ Destination: IPv6mcast_ff:a3:f4:69 (33:33:ff:a3:f4:69)
    Address: IPv6mcast_ff:a3:f4:69 (33:33:ff:a3:f4:69)
    .... ..1. .... = LG bit: Locally administered address (this is NOT the factory default)
    ....1 .... = IG bit: Group address (multicast/broadcast)
  ⊟ Source: Wistron_0b:b0:92 (00:16:d3:0b:b0:92)
    Address: Wistron_0b:b0:92 (00:16:d3:0b:b0:92)
    .... ..0. .... = LG bit: Globally unique address (factory default)
    ....0 .... = IG bit: Individual address (unicast)
  Type: IPv6 (0x86dd)
⊟ Internet Protocol Version 6, Src: :: (::), Dst: ff02::1:ffa3:f469 (ff02::1:ffa3:f469)
  ⊟ 0110 .... = Version: 6
    [0110 .... = This field makes the filter "ip.version == 6" possible: 6]
  ⊟ .... 0000 0000 .... = Traffic class: 0x00000000
    .... 0000 00.. .... = Differentiated Services Field: Default (0x00000000)
    ....0. .... = ECN-Capable Transport (ECT): Not set
    ....0 .... = ECN-CE: Not set
    .... 0000 0000 0000 0000 0000 = Flowlabel: 0x00000000
  Payload length: 24
  Next header: ICMPv6 (58)
  Hop limit: 255
  Source: :: (::)
  Destination: ff02::1:ffa3:f469 (ff02::1:ffa3:f469)
  [Source GeoIP: Unknown]
  [Destination GeoIP: Unknown]
⊟ Internet Control Message Protocol v6
  Type: Neighbor Solicitation (135)
  Code: 0
  Checksum: 0x0d46 [correct]
  Reserved: 00000000
  Target Address: fe80::a5c2:b004:2fa3:f469 (fe80::a5c2:b004:2fa3:f469)

Figure 78a

⊞ Frame 12: 78 bytes on wire (624 bits), 78 bytes captured (624 bits) on interface 0
⊟ Ethernet II, Src: Wistron_0b:b0:92 (00:16:d3:0b:b0:92), Dst: IPv6mcast_ff:a3:f4:69 (33:33:ff:a3:f4:69)
  ⊟ Destination: IPv6mcast_ff:a3:f4:69 (33:33:ff:a3:f4:69)
    Address: IPv6mcast_ff:a3:f4:69 (33:33:ff:a3:f4:69)
    .... ..1. .... = LG bit: Locally administered address (this is NOT the factory default)
    ....1 .... = IG bit: Group address (multicast/broadcast)
  ⊟ Source: Wistron_0b:b0:92 (00:16:d3:0b:b0:92)
    Address: Wistron_0b:b0:92 (00:16:d3:0b:b0:92)
    .... ..0. .... = LG bit: Globally unique address (factory default)
    ....0 .... = IG bit: Individual address (unicast)
  Type: IPv6 (0x86dd)
⊞ Internet Protocol Version 6, Src: :: (::), Dst: ff02::1:ffa3:f469 (ff02::1:ffa3:f469)

Figure 78b: Header Ethernet II (IEEE 802.3)

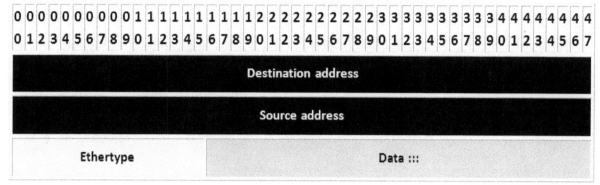

Figure 78c: Ethernet II Header

Figures 78b and 78c illustrate the ethernet II header. Inside the ethernet 11 headers contains information about the next upper level protocol which is 0x86dd for is IPv6, as shown in the next to last line in Figure 78b. The contents of each field of Ethernet II header in Figure 78c is explained below.

- **Destination Address.** 6 byte (48 bit): This is the destination MAC address. It can be a unicast address, multicast or broadcast.
- **Source Address.** 6 byte (48 bit): It is the source MAC address of the hosts sending the message.
- **Ethertype.** 2 byte (16 bit): This field specifies the next protocol that follows. A value of 0x86dd refers to IPv6.
- **Data.** The minimum size for data is 46 byte while the maximum is 1500 byte.

Reference
https://www.ietf.org/rfc/rfc3315.txt
https://tools.ietf.org/html/rfc4443
http://www.ietf.org/rfc/rfc2461.txt
https://www.ietf.org/rfc/rfc2710.txt
https://tools.ietf.org/html/rfc3810

Chapter 10
BOOT UP

- The Boot Up Process
- Duplicate Address Detection
- Router Advertisement
- Router Advertisement Interval
- Router Solicitation
- Neighbor Solicitation
- Multicast Listener Discovery (MLD)
- Neighbor Advertisement

THE BOOT UP PROCESS

Every IPv6 host will need to go through the following process before all the resources on the network are accessible. Explanation on each step of the process is explained in this chapter in detail.

1. Duplicate Address Detection (LLA): ICMPv6 Neighbor Solicitation
2. Router Discovery: ICMPv6 Router Solicitation
3. Router Advertisement: ICMPv6 Router Advertisement
4. Neighbor Discovery: ICMPv6 Neighbor Solicitation
5. Neighbor Advertisement: ICMPv6 Neighbor Advertisement
6. Duplicate Address Detection (GUA): ICMPv6 Neighbor Solicitation

The explanation in this chapter refers to an IPv6 host with the following configuration:
- Local-link scope all-nodes address (Destination: FF02::1) – Neighbor Solicitation.
- Solicited-node multicast address (Destination: FF02::1:FF28:9C5A) – Neighbor Solicitation.
- Link-local IPv6 address of FE80::2AA:FF:FE28:9C5A.

DUPLICATE ADDRESS DETECTION (DAD)

The purpose of duplicate address detection is to ensure that an IPv6 address configured on a host is unique before activated on any network interface. DAD will initiate in any one of the following situation:

a. The network interface of a host is connected to a wireless network or wired network.
b. An IPv6 host receives a router advertisement (RA) with a different prefix other than the one it's currently using.

The following is the DAD process explained in sequence.

a. A host will join the "link local all node multicast group" (FF02::1) once its interface is activated. An IP address of FF02::1 will be made active on the host interface. This can be seen clearly once the MAC address of the host is filtered with Wireshark. A filter of "**eth.src == 00:25:84:f4:1b:69**" would fulfill such purpose.

b. The host will join the "solicited-node multicast group" for the local address. Every host with a unicast or multicast address will have to join the "solicited node multicast group". The solicited-node multicast address prefix is FF02::1:FF00:0/104 combined with the last 24 bit from the IPv6 address that will be used by the host. An example of solicited-node address is a destination of: FF02::1:FF28:9C5A for an IPv6 address of FE80::2AA:FF:FE28:9C5A.

c. The host will then send a neighbor solicitation to the solicited node multicast address that contains the IPv6 address that it wishes to use. The host sends a packet destination of FF02::1:FF28:9C5A for an IP address of FE80::2AA:FF:FE28:9C5A. The source IP address is "::". This message can be seen in packet number 18 in Figure 79a.

d. The host waits for a response from other hosts in the network.

e. If there is no response from any hosts, the address is considered unique and valid to be made active on the host.

f. In the situation where there is a response from other hosts, the address considered isn't unique. The host will exit from the "solicited-node multicast group" and a balloon appears with message "duplicate address detected" on the users desktop.

g. The entire process from a to f will be repeated again for ULA or GUA as seen in Figure 79a packet number 23.

No.	Time	Source	Destination	Protocol	Length	Info
18	20.0887200	::	ff02::1:ffa3:f469	ICMPv6	78	Neighbor Solicitation for fe80::a5c2:b004:2fa3:f469
19	20.0887260	fe80::a5c2:b004:2fa3:f469	ff02::2	ICMPv6	70	Router Solicitation from 00:16:d3:0b:b0:92
20	20.0887730	fe80::a5c2:b004:2fa3:f469	ff02::16	ICMPv6	90	Multicast Listener Report Message v2
22	20.0931220	fe80::a5c2:b004:2fa3:f469	ff02::16	ICMPv6	90	Multicast Listener Report Message v2
23	20.5918550	::	ff02::1:ffa3:f469	ICMPv6	78	Neighbor Solicitation for fa00:1::a5c2:b004:2fa3:f469
24	20.5918630	::	ff02::1:ff1c:e90b	ICMPv6	78	Neighbor Solicitation for fa00:1::fdc9:97f9:e61c:e90b
25	20.5919100	fe80::a5c2:b004:2fa3:f469	ff02::16	ICMPv6	110	Multicast Listener Report Message v2
29	25.8212560	fe80::a5c2:b004:2fa3:f469	ff02::16	ICMPv6	90	Multicast Listener Report Message v2
30	25.8239950	fe80::a5c2:b004:2fa3:f469	ff02::16	ICMPv6	90	Multicast Listener Report Message v2
31	25.8375050	fe80::a5c2:b004:2fa3:f469	ff02::16	ICMPv6	90	Multicast Listener Report Message v2

Filter: eth.src == 00:16:d3:0b:b0:92

Figure 79a

No.	Time	Source	Destination	Protocol	Length	Info
18	20.0887200	::	ff02::1:ffa3:f469	ICMPv6	78	Neighbor Solicitation for fe80::a5c2:b004:2fa3:f469

⊞ Frame 18: 78 bytes on wire (624 bits), 78 bytes captured (624 bits) on interface 0
⊞ Ethernet II, Src: Wistron_0b:b0:92 (00:16:d3:0b:b0:92), Dst: IPv6mcast_ff:a3:f4:69 (33:33:ff:a3:f4:69)
⊞ Internet Protocol Version 6, Src: :: (::), Dst: ff02::1:ffa3:f469 (ff02::1:ffa3:f469)
⊟ Internet Control Message Protocol v6
   Type: Neighbor Solicitation (135)
   Code: 0
   Checksum: 0x0d46 [correct]
   Reserved: 00000000
   Target Address: fe80::a5c2:b004:2fa3:f469 (fe80::a5c2:b004:2fa3:f469)

Figure 79b

Figure 79b shows frame number 18 with a destination address fe80::a5c2:b004:2fa3:fa69. The purpose here is to determine the uniqueness of the address before the address is activated on a host interface.

Note: The two main categories of neighbor solicitation that need to be differentiated between one another is the neighbor solicitation where the info column shows "**neighbor solicitation for <IPv6 address>**" and the other is "**neighbor solicitation for <IPv6 address> from <IPv6 address>**". The "Neighbor solicitation for <IPv6 address> is used for the purpose of avoiding address conflicts where as "Neighbor solicitation for <IPv6 address> from <IPv6 address> is a communication message to obtain the MAC address based on an IPv6 address of host that is destined to be the destination transmission. The filter of "ipv6.dst== ff02::1:ffa3:f469 || ipv6.dst == ff02::1:fff4:1b69" for Wireshark can isolate both types of traffic. Refer to Figure 79c.

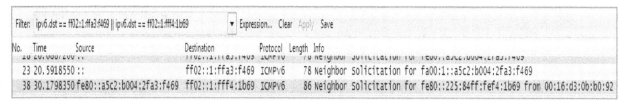

Figure 79c

ROUTER ADVERTISEMENT (RA)

- Frame No. 91 from router IPv6.

- Source IPv6 address: Router Link Local (fe80::225:84ff:fef4:1b69)

- Destination IPv6 address: Multicast

- Destination Multicast address: FF02:0:0:0:0:0:0:1 (All node in the scope of link local)

- Protocol ICMPv6: Type: 134 ,Code: 0

- Interval: Every 200 seconds

- Purpose: To announce the network prefix for all the hosts in that particular network.

Refer to Figure 80a. A Router advertisement message contains the network prefix that should be used by all hosts. It is the path or way out to other networks acting as the gateway address for each host. Besides containing the network prefix the router advertisement also contains other configuration information such as the M flag and the O flag that will be explained in greater detail in the upcoming chapters.

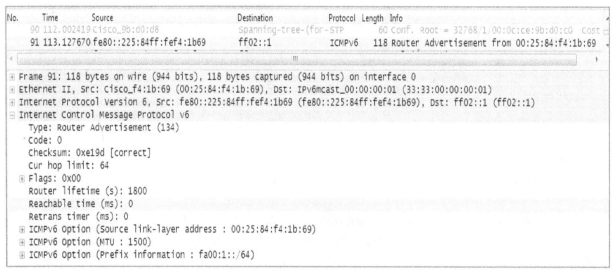

Figure 80a

As at of this writing RA can only sent out by the latest IPv6 routers and server operating systems. A router advertisement will only be produced by a router that is configured with an IPv6 address. In Figure 80a, frame number 91 shows the Internet Control Message Protocol version 6 headers that are encapsulated in the Internet Protocol version 6 while the Internet

Protocol Version 6 is encapsulated in Ethernet II. The last row shows that inside the ICMPv6 is an information of the prefix as indicated in the "Prefix information: fa00:1::/64".

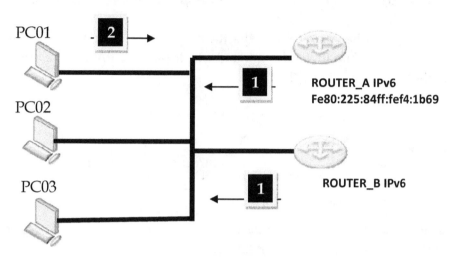

Figure 80b

1	**ROUTER ADVERTISEMENT**	A multicast from ROUTER_A contains the information about the network prefix that is to be used in the LAN. .
2	**ROUTER SOLICITATION**	Host PC01 sends a multicast asking for a local router to respond with a router advertisement for the IPv6 configuration.
CONCLUSION: A router will send out router advertisement messages at specific intervals. There is the possibility that the router might receive a router solicitation before it sends out router advertisement.		

Figure 80c

```
RTRlatiffesa#show ipv6 interface
FastEthernet0/1 is up, line protocol is down
  IPv6 is tentative, link-local address is FE80::225:84FF:FEF4:1B69 [TEN]
  No Virtual link-local address(es):
  Global unicast address(es):
    FA00:1::225:84FF:FEF4:1B69, subnet is FA00:1::/64 [EUI/TEN]
  Joined group address(es):
    FF02::1
    FF02::2
  MTU is 1500 bytes
  ICMP error messages limited to one every 100 milliseconds
  ICMP redirects are enabled
  ICMP unreachables are sent
  ND DAD is enabled, number of DAD attempts: 1
  ND reachable time is 30000 milliseconds (using 30000)
  ND advertised reachable time is 0 (unspecified)
  ND advertised retransmit interval is 0 (unspecified)
  ND router advertisements are sent every 200 seconds
  ND router advertisements live for 1800 seconds
  ND advertised default router preference is Medium
  Hosts use stateless autoconfig for addresses.
```

Figure 81

ROUTER ADVERTISEMENT INTERVAL

There are situations where the network setup requires that router's RA need to be disabled. This would nicely fit in a WAN interface configuration setup. The following will display the current router's advertisement interval with the *show ipv6 interface command*.

Determine the RA interval before disabling the RA on a router interface with the "*ipv6 nd ra surpress*" command. The *debug ipv6 nd* command will display the RA transmission that is active on the current interface. Refer Figure 81a.

```
*Feb 28 23:47:04.123: ICMPv6-ND: Sending RA from FE80::225:84FF:FEF4:1B69 to FF0
2::1 on FastEthernet0/1
*Feb 28 23:47:04.123: ICMPv6-ND:      MTU = 1500
*Feb 28 23:47:04.123: ICMPv6-ND:      prefix = FA00:1::/64 onlink autoconfig
*Feb 28 23:47:04.123: ICMPv6-ND:          2592000/604800 (valid/preferred)
*Feb 28 23:47:04.127: ICMPv6-ND: ND output feature SEND executed on 3 - rc=0
```

Figure 81a

The *ipv6 nd ra surpress* command should be used on the interface prompt. Figure 81b shows that no RA output is seen, that is "ND router advertisement".

```
RTRlatiffesa(config-if)#do show ipv6 int
FastEthernet0/1 is up, line protocol is up
  IPv6 is enabled, link-local address is FE80::225:84FF:FEF4:1B69
  No Virtual link-local address(es):
  Global unicast address(es):
    FA00:1::225:84FF:FEF4:1B69, subnet is FA00:1::/64 [EUI]
  Joined group address(es):
    FF02::1
    FF02::2
    FF02::1:FFF4:1B69
  MTU is 1500 bytes
  ICMP error messages limited to one every 100 milliseconds
  ICMP redirects are enabled
  ICMP unreachables are sent
  ND DAD is enabled, number of DAD attempts: 1
  ND reachable time is 30000 milliseconds (using 30000)
  Hosts use stateless autoconfig for addresses.
```

Figure 81b

ROUTER SOLICITATION (Protocol ICMPv6: Type 133 code 0)

- Frame 19 from Windows 7 operating system.
- Destination: FE02::2 (Multicast – All router in the scope of link local)
- Source: Windows 7 (winstron_0b:b0:92/00:16:d3:0b:b0:92)

Router Solicitation messages are sent at preset intervals. Microsoft Windows 7 and 8 will send out router solicitation messages every time they boot up if IPv6 is active on the interface.

Figures 81c to 84 show that during boot up PC01 sends out multicast in order to obtain a response from the router for a network prefix. Figure 82 show that both routers will respond with an RA.

No.	Time	Source	Destination	Protocol	Length	Info
19	20.0887260	fe80::a5c2:b004:2fa3:f469	ff02::2	ICMPv6	70	Router Solicitation from 00:16:d3:0b:b0:92

```
⊞ Frame 19: 70 bytes on wire (560 bits), 70 bytes captured (560 bits) on interface 0
⊞ Ethernet II, Src: Wistron_0b:b0:92 (00:16:d3:0b:b0:92), Dst: IPv6mcast_00:00:00:02 (33:33:00:00:00:02)
⊞ Internet Protocol Version 6, Src: fe80::a5c2:b004:2fa3:f469 (fe80::a5c2:b004:2fa3:f469), Dst: ff02::2 (ff02::2)
⊟ Internet Control Message Protocol v6
    Type: Router Solicitation (133)
    Code: 0
    Checksum: 0x7ea5 [correct]
    Reserved: 00000000
  ⊟ ICMPv6 Option (Source link-layer address : 00:16:d3:0b:b0:92)
      Type: Source link-layer address (1)
      Length: 1 (8 bytes)
      Link-layer address: Wistron_0b:b0:92 (00:16:d3:0b:b0:92)
```

Figure 81c

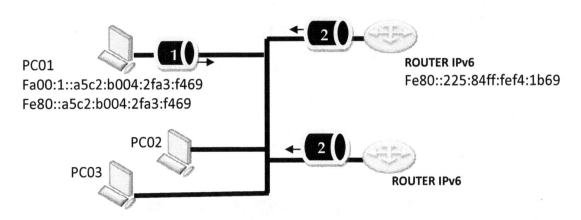

PC01
Fa00:1::a5c2:b004:2fa3:f469
Fe80::a5c2:b004:2fa3:f469

PC02

PC03

ROUTER IPv6
Fe80::225:84ff:fef4:1b69

ROUTER IPv6

Figure 82: When there is more than one router, you can't control
which router will accept the RA.

1	**ROUTER SOLICITATION**	PC01 sends a multicast from the local router asking for an RA that contains the prefix.
2	**ROUTER ADVERTISEMENT**	Router(s) will respond with an RA with a prefix allocation for the network.
CONCLUSION: When a computer boots up it will send out a router solicitation message. In response, it will receive a router advertisement message. There is the possibility that the computer might receive a router advertisement before it sends out router solicitation.		

Figure 83

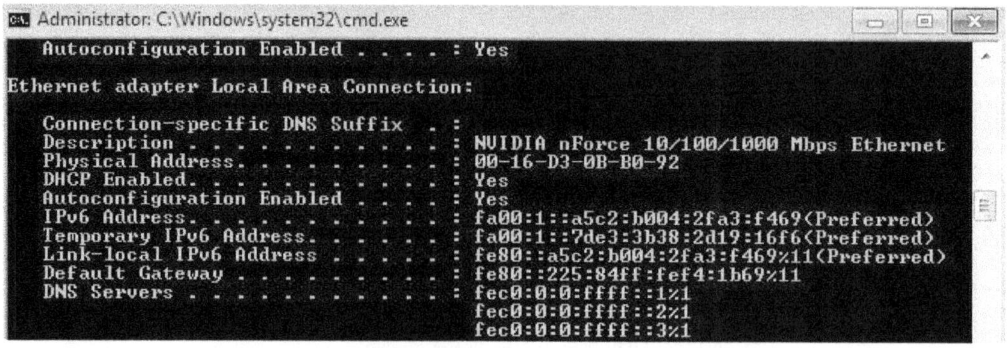

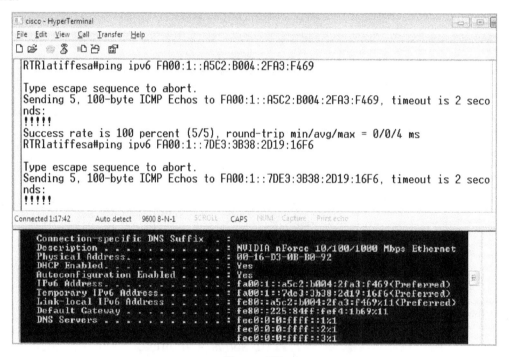

Figure 84: Screen shot

A test ping to both the computers, PC01 and PC02, was successful using the "***ping ipv6***" command.

Figure 85

A test ping from the router to the IPv6 link local address of the computer was also successful. Refer to Figure 86.

```
RTRlatiffesa#ping ipv6 Fe80::a5c2:b004:2fa3:f469
Output Interface: fastethernet0/1
Type escape sequence to abort.
Sending 5, 100-byte ICMP Echos to FE80::A5C2:B004:2FA3:F469, timeout is 2 second
s:
Packet sent with a source address of FE80::225:84FF:FEF4:1B69%FastEthernet0/1
!!!!!
Success rate is 100 percent (5/5), round-trip min/avg/max = 0/0/4 ms
```

Figure 86

NEIGHBOR SOLICITATION (NS)

- Packet type: Multicast
- Destination: FF02::1:ffa3:f469

- Purpose: The purpose of this communication is to avoid IP address conflicts and to identify other hosts' link layer addresses that are in the same link. Refer to Figure 87. The neighbor cache can be displayed using the ***netsh int ipv6 show neigh*** command.

Frame number 104 which is a neighbor solicitation from Windows 7 (source: mac 00:16:d3:0b:b0:92) shows a multicast communication to a destination address of ff02::1:ffa3:f469. The purpose of this multicast is to announce its intention to use the IPv6 address of fa001::a5c2:b004:2fa3:f469. This methodology is a beneficial way to avoid IP address conflicts. Another advantage of IPv6 is has the option to make use of a host's mac address as part of the IP address to serve the same purpose too. Refer to Figures 73 and 92 on the various types of Neighbor Discovery Protocol (NDP).

```
No.     Time      Source          Destination       Protocol Length Info
   104 113.463557 ::              ff02::1:ffa3:f469 ICMPv6   78 Neighbor Solicitation for fa00:1::a5c2:b004:2fa3:f469

⊞ Frame 104: 78 bytes on wire (624 bits), 78 bytes captured (624 bits) on interface 0
⊞ Ethernet II, Src: Wistron_0b:b0:92 (00:16:d3:0b:b0:92), Dst: IPv6mcast_ff:a3:f4:69 (33:33:ff:a3:f4:69)
⊞ Internet Protocol Version 6, Src: :: (::), Dst: ff02::1:ffa3:f469 (ff02::1:ffa3:f469)
⊟ Internet Control Message Protocol v6
    Type: Neighbor Solicitation (135)
    Code: 0
    Checksum: 0x11c5 [correct]
    Reserved: 00000000
    Target Address: fa00:1::a5c2:b004:2fa3:f469 (fa00:1::a5c2:b004:2fa3:f469)
```

Figure 87

Refer to Figure 89a. The ***netsh*** command shows that the IPv6 *address* of the router Fa00:1::225:84ff:fef4:1b69 and fe80::225:84ff:fef4:1b69 is a neighbor to that computer. It is a result from the neighbor solicitation message. The same screen capture also shows that the computer is also a member of several multicast groups (FF02::2, FF02::c and FF02::16).

MULTICAST LISTENER DISCOVERY (MLD)

FF02::16 Multicast Link Local Scope. It is a type of multicast that is limited to the local-link. The multicast address is addressed to all link scope all-MLDv2 routers that are within the subnet. This multicast is not the same as FF02::2 (refer to Figure 30). MLD version 2 is meant for routers with MLDv2 capability. MLD version 2 has the capability to carry more group information in one transmission report with a destination multicast address of FF02::16. The acronym "local link" refers to Ethernet LAN. By default, all routers will not allow this type of multicast to pass through their *interface*. The multicast FF02::16 will be limited to the scope of link local. The multicast address of FF02::16 will only be sent by hosts that are a member of "solicited node multicast group". Refer to the following table. It is one of the multicasts categorized under MLD (Multicast Listener Discovery). An explanation on all the three types of MLD is explained in the following table (Figure 88).

MULTICAST: MLD (Multicast Listener Discovery)	
Multicast Listener Query	<ul><li>It is a message from a router to other host.</li><li>It is a message from a router to the entire subnet to identify all the hosts that are in the same multicast group known as multicast listeners.</li></ul>

	• There are two types of listener queries and are differentiated by destination multicast addresses; they are: a. General Query: Used to query multicast listeners of all multicast address b. Specific Query: Used to query multicast listeners of a specific multicast address • In a network with multiple routers, only one router will send MLD query messages. A querier election will elect the router with the lowest IP address as the querier while the others are non queriers.
Multicast Listener Report	• It is a message from a host to router. • It is in response to the multicast listener query from a router. • It is sent from a host that is a member of the multicast group query. • If the router does not receive a response, the router will stop any further query for that multicast group.
Multicast Listener Done	• It is a message from a host to a router. The host is leaving the group and it is the last member in the group. • The destination address is ff02::2, that is, to all routers.

Figure 88

```
C:\Users\latiffesa123>netsh int ipv6 show neigh

Interface 1: Loopback Pseudo-Interface 1


Internet Address                                Physical Address    Type
--------------------------------------------    ----------------    -----------
ff02::c                                                             Permanent
ff02::16                                                            Permanent

Interface 11: Local Area Connection


Internet Address                                Physical Address    Type
--------------------------------------------    ----------------    -----------
fa00:1::225:84ff:fef4:1b69                      00-25-84-f4-1b-69   Stale (Router)
fe80::225:84ff:fef4:1b69                        00-25-84-f4-1b-69   Reachable (Rout
er)
ff02::2                                         33-33-00-00-00-02   Permanent
ff02::c                                         33-33-00-00-00-0c   Permanent
ff02::16                                        33-33-00-00-00-16   Permanent
ff02::1:3                                       33-33-00-01-00-03   Permanent
ff02::1:ff19:16f6                               33-33-ff-19-16-f6   Permanent
ff02::1:ffa3:f469                               33-33-ff-a3-f4-69   Permanent
ff02::1:fff4:1b69                               33-33-ff-f4-1b-69   Permanent

Interface 14: Teredo Tunneling Pseudo-Interface


Internet Address                                Physical Address    Type
--------------------------------------------    ----------------    -----------
ff02::16                                        255.255.255.255:65535  Permanent
```

Figure 89a

```
No.  Time       Source                  Destination        Protocol  Length  Info
 22 20.0931220 fe80::a5c2:b004:2fa3:f469 ff02::16          ICMPv6    90 Multicast Listener Report Message v2
```

⊞ Frame 22: 90 bytes on wire (720 bits), 90 bytes captured (720 bits) on interface 0
⊞ Ethernet II, Src: Wistron_0b:b0:92 (00:16:d3:0b:b0:92), Dst: IPv6mcast_00:00:00:16 (33:33:00:00:00:16)
⊞ Internet Protocol Version 6, Src: fe80::a5c2:b004:2fa3:f469 (fe80::a5c2:b004:2fa3:f469), Dst: ff02::16 (ff02::16)
⊟ Internet Control Message Protocol v6
    Type: Multicast Listener Report Message v2 (143)
    Code: 0
    Checksum: 0x0e0d [correct]
    Reserved: 0000
    Number of Multicast Address Records: 1
⊟ Multicast Address Record Changed to exclude: ff02::1:ff1c:e90b
    Record Type: Changed to exclude (4)
    Aux Data Len: 0
    Number of Sources: 0
    Multicast Address: ff02::1:ff1c:e90b (ff02::1:ff1c:e90b)

Figure 89

NEIGHBOUR ADVERTISEMENT (NA)

Neighbour Advertisement (NA) is another multicast communication categorized under the Neighbor Discovery Protocol (NDP). NDP uses ICMPv6 for many purposes. NA uses ICMP type 136 with a destination address of address FF02::1. The "FF" Character indicates that it is a multicast and "02" refers to link local address. Among others, the purpose of NA is as follows:

- To identify the link layer address of other hosts that are in the same link; that is the same as what ARP is for in IPv4.

- To identify neighbors that are active.

NEIGHBOR SOLICITATION: Frame No. 5 ICMPv6 Type 135 Code 0 Source: fe80::225:84ff:fef4:1b69 Source MAC: 00:25.84:f4.1b:69 Destination: fe80::a5c2:b004:2fa3:f469 Dst MAC: 00:16:d3:0b:b0:92 Router querying for link address Windows 7	**NEIGHBOR ADVERTISEMENT**: Frame No.6 ICMPv6 Type 136 Code 0 Source: fe80::a5c2:b004:2fa3: f469 Source MAC: 00:16:d3:0b:b0:92 Destination: fe80::225:84ff:fef4:1b69 Dst MAC: 00:25.84:f4.1b:69 Windows 7 responded to the routers request.

Figure 90 shows an NS and an NA frame. The Neighbor Solicitation from fe80::225:84ff:fef4:1b69 to fe80:a5c2:b004:2fa3:f469 is followed by a reply of Neighbor Advertisement from fe80:a5c2:b004:2fa3:f469 to fe80::225:84ff:fef4:1b69. Both the hosts are exchanging information regarding their link layer address (mac address) with one another. Neighbor Advertisement will only take place for hosts that are in the same link. Refer to Figure 91. Once the router receives the link layer address, the router will keep the information gathered in a neighbor cache. The contents of the neighbor cache can be displayed with the "**sh ipv6 neighbor**" command on a router or "**netsh int ipv6 show nei**" command on Windows 7 operating systems.

```
Time        Source                    Destination              Protocol Length Info
5 0.04849500 fe80::225:84ff:fef4:1b69 fe80::a5c2:b004:2fa3:f469 ICMPv6   86 Neighbor Solicitation for fe80::a5c2:b004:2fa3:f
6 0.04866100 fe80::a5c2:b004:2fa3:f469 fe80::225:84ff:fef4:1b69 ICMPv6   86 Neighbor Advertisement fe80::a5c2:b004:2fa3:f469
                                                    III

⊞ Frame 6: 86 bytes on wire (688 bits), 86 bytes captured (688 bits) on interface 0
⊞ Ethernet II, Src: Wistron_0b:b0:92 (00:16:d3:0b:b0:92), Dst: Cisco_f4:1b:69 (00:25:84:f4:1b:69)
⊞ Internet Protocol Version 6, Src: fe80::a5c2:b004:2fa3:f469 (fe80::a5c2:b004:2fa3:f469), Dst: fe80::225:84ff:fef4:1b69 (fe80:
⊟ Internet Control Message Protocol v6
    Type: Neighbor Advertisement (136)
    Code: 0
    Checksum: 0x0141 [correct]
  ⊞ Flags: 0x60000000
    Target Address: fe80::a5c2:b004:2fa3:f469 (fe80::a5c2:b004:2fa3:f469)
  ⊟ ICMPv6 Option (Target link-layer address : 00:16:d3:0b:b0:92)
      Type: Target link-layer address (2)
      Length: 1 (8 bytes)
      Link-layer address: Wistron_0b:b0:92 (00:16:d3:0b:b0:92)
```

```
Time        Source                    Destination              Protocol Length Info
5 0.04849500 fe80::225:84ff:fef4:1b69 fe80::a5c2:b004:2fa3:f469 ICMPv6   86 Neighbor Solicitation for fe80::a5c2:b004:2fa3:f
6 0.04866100 fe80::a5c2:b004:2fa3:f469 fe80::225:84ff:fef4:1b69 ICMPv6   86 Neighbor Advertisement fe80::a5c2:b004:2fa3:f469
                                                    III

⊞ Frame 5: 86 bytes on wire (688 bits), 86 bytes captured (688 bits) on interface 0
⊞ Ethernet II, Src: Cisco_f4:1b:69 (00:25:84:f4:1b:69), Dst: Wistron_0b:b0:92 (00:16:d3:0b:b0:92)
⊞ Internet Protocol Version 6, Src: fe80::225:84ff:fef4:1b69 (fe80::225:84ff:fef4:1b69), Dst: fe80::a5c2:b004:2fa3:f469 (fe80:
⊟ Internet Control Message Protocol v6
    Type: Neighbor Solicitation (135)
    Code: 0
    Checksum: 0x4673 [correct]
    Reserved: 00000000
    Target Address: fe80::a5c2:b004:2fa3:f469 (fe80::a5c2:b004:2fa3:f469)
  ⊟ ICMPv6 Option (Source link-layer address : 00:25:84:f4:1b:69)
      Type: Source link-layer address (1)
      Length: 1 (8 bytes)
      Link-layer address: Cisco_f4:1b:69 (00:25:84:f4:1b:69)
```

Figure 90

1	NEIGHBOR SOLICITATION	Which host is using this IPv6 address? Please update me on your link address.
2	NEIIGHBOR ADVERTISEMENT	I am the host with that IPv6 address; this is my link layer address.

CONCLUSION: After a computer boots up and confirms its IPv6 address, it will send out a neighbor solicitation message and in response it will receive neighbor advertisement from other hosts. There is also a possibility that a host will receive a neighbor advertisement even before it sends out the neighbor solicitation.

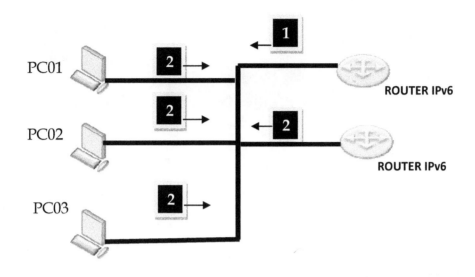

Figure 91

THE PURPOSE OF NEIGHBOR DISCOVERY PROTOCOL (NDP)		
NO	**CATEGORY**	**EXPLANATION**
1	**HOST**	To identify the status of other hosts on the network including computers and routers.
		To obtain network prefix and other network configuration.
2	**ROUTER**	To multicast its existence in the existing network.
		To inform other hosts of availability of another host that is better for reaching a specific destination network.
3	**HOST AND ROUTER**	To obtain the link layer address (MAC address) before using the network layer communication methodology (address IPv6).
		To identify if a host is an IPv6 capable device.

Figure 92

Reference
https://tools.ietf.org/html/rfc4862
https://tools.ietf.org/html/rfc4861
https://tools.ietf.org/html/rfc5175
https://tools.ietf.org/html/rfc4861
http://www.rfc-editor.org/rfc/rfc3122.txt

Chapter 11
DHCPv6

Dynamic Host Configuration Protocol (DHCP) is used to assign hosts with IP addresses and prefixes and other configuration data required to operate in a network. IPv6 hosts may automatically generate addresses, etc using *stateless* auto configuration, or they may be assigned configuration data with DCHPv6.

STATEFUL & STATELESS

In computer terms the word *stateful* means to monitor the entire communication session from the start right until the end at session termination. Whereas *stateless* means "not to keep track of its state". A *stateless* program does not keep track of any changes which relates to configuration or transactions. Such program would not relate the last session to the next.

On the other hand *stateful* would nicely fit in an organization where the IP address management is very critical. Stateful is the opposite of stateless. Stateful would monitor and can relate one session to the next. It is similar to DHCP in IPv4 that requires the DHCP server to keep track of address assignments to clients and its duration. DHCP in IPv6 is known as DHCPv6 and it requires a server operating system.

The Microsoft Windows Server 2008 needs to be configured as *"Disable DHCPv6 stateless mode for this server"* during DHCP setup in order to function as stateful. Such configuration will allow the IPv6 clients to obtain the prefix for the current network but without the DNS configuration. Whether you choose to activate stateful or stateless on Windows Server 2008 and 2012, your configuration needs to match with the current router setup in order for everything to work. Verify the existing DHCP clients configuration with all five commands listed below:

netsh int ipv6 show int [index]	• Verify the current configuration
netsh int ipv6 set int [index] routerdiscovery=disabled	• Disable the routerdiscovery configuration.
netsh int ipv6 set int [index] routerdiscovery=enabled	• Enable the routerdiscovery configuration in order to obtain the prefix and gateway.
netsh int ipv6 set int [index] managedaddress=disabled	• Disable the managedaddress configuration.
netsh int ipv6 set int [index] managedaddress=enabled	• Enable the managedaddress configuration in order to obtain the DNS Ip address configuration.

Substitute the [index] and the [Idx] value from the output of the *"**netsh int ipv6 show int**"* command. The word "Ldx" refers to the unique number allocated to each interface (see Figure 93). (Later in the Chapter, the summary of the default setup for each client configuration is shown in Figure 113.)

```
C:\>netsh int ipv6 show int
 Idx    Met    MTU       State        Name
 ---    -----  --------  ----------   ------------------------
  1     50     4294967295  connected    Loopback Pseudo-Interface 1
 35     25     1500        connected    Wireless Network Connection
 39     25     1280        connected    isatap.Home
 54     25     1280        connected    isatap.{92832363-B825-497E-B3BF-5579F5756062}
 23     25     1280        connected    isatap.{8DB357C6-251C-4AEB-BBE5-
109546409AA2}
 12     10     1500        disconnected  Local Area Connection
 13     50     1280        disconnected  Teredo Tunneling Pseudo-Interface
```

Figure 93: the *netsh int ipv6 show interface* command output shows that each interface is assigned an "Idx" identification number

FLAG M & FLAG O

It is important to match the router RA configuration with the Windows Server 2012 operating system running DHCPv6 along with the "Managed and Other" configuration on the DHCP client's operating system settings. All three setups should be coordinated to make everything work. On the device router the two options for the RA bit flag is the M flag and the O flag. Referring to Figure 94, There are several combination options for both flags. The M flag is configured with the *"nd managed-config-flag"* option whereas the O flag is configured wit the *"nd other-config-flag"*. A Router with the M flag activated will send out ICMPv6 multicast with the M flag set to 1.

Figure 95 shows the Wireshark application with frame number 139 where the source address is fe80::225:84ff:fef4:1b68 with a destination address of ff02::1. There is a high possibility that the combination of M=1/O=0 (M1O0) and M=0/O=0 (M0O0) will not be used at all.

Referring again to Figure 94, most networks will make use of either M0O1 or M1O1. The M0O1 flag which is stateless will setup the DHCP clients to obtain their prefix from router and their DNS configurations from the DHCPv6 servers. Each and every DHCP client will be allocated the prefix, default gateway and preferred DNS configurations for the network access.

The M1O1 flag is known as stateful. The M1O1 setup will setup the DHCP clients to obtain both their IPv6 address and preferred DNS from a DHCPv6 server (server 2012/Server 2008). It is important to note that the M1O1 will not allocate the default gateway configuration if the router is not configured to issue RA. It is important to coordinate the M1O1 on the clients with the M's and O's flag in the RA from the router. As of this writing there is no option to configure the Server 2012 and Server 2008 servers to transmit RA. The only host that is capable to transmit RA is routers.

ROUTER FLAG **M** and **FLAG O**			
FLAG	**EXPLANATION**	**ROUTER**	**Windows 7 & Windows 8**
M = 1 **O = 0**	DHCPv6 is used for the entire IPv6 address configuration.	R1(config-if)# ipv6 **nd managed-config-flag**	Clients will only obtain the IPv6 addresses from DHCPv6. Preferred DNS configuration needs to be done manually on the clients. The clients will obtain the default gateway addresses from the router. High possibility that this kind of setup will not be used.
M = 0 **O = 1** *	**STATELESS** (SLAAC): The purpose is to use autoconfig for IPv6 address. Other configuration will require a DHCPv6. (Figure 106)	R1(config-if)# ipv6 **nd other-config-flag**	Clients will only obtain the IPv6 addresses from router. DHCPv6 is required for preferred DNS configuration. SLAAC means **Stateless Address Auto Configuration.**

*Notes
- The M0O1 configuration would meet the requirements of most IPv6 LAN networks.
- Windows 7 and Windows 8 require no configuration.
- Windows Server 2012 will require the "options" configurations for clients DNS.
- Router activates the network prefix and act as the gateway.

M = 1 **O = 1** **	**STATEFUL**: DHCPv6 is used for IPv6 address and DNS configuration. **There will be no Internet access if RA ROUTER is not configured with RA.**	R1(config-if)# ipv6 **nd managed-config-flag** R1(config-if)# ipv6 **nd other-config-flag**	IPv6 address and DNS configurations from DHCPv6. Gateway configurations from the router RA.

**Notes:
- The M1O1 configuration would meet the requirements of most IPv6 LAN networks.
- Windows 7 and Windows 8 require no configuration.
- Server 2012 requires DHCPv6 configuration for clients IPv6 address and preferred DNS.
- Router requires the M and 0 flag activated.
- DHCP clients will obtain an IPv6 address and preferred DNS address from DHCPv6, and the default gateway address from the router.

M = 0 **O = 0**	Without the use of DHCPv6 there will be no Internet access unless a proxy server is setup.	**DEFAULT** Refer to Figure 109.	Clients will only receive network prefix and default gateway setup. DNS configuration is done manually on the clients.

Figure 94: Summary reference table for M and O flag combinations.

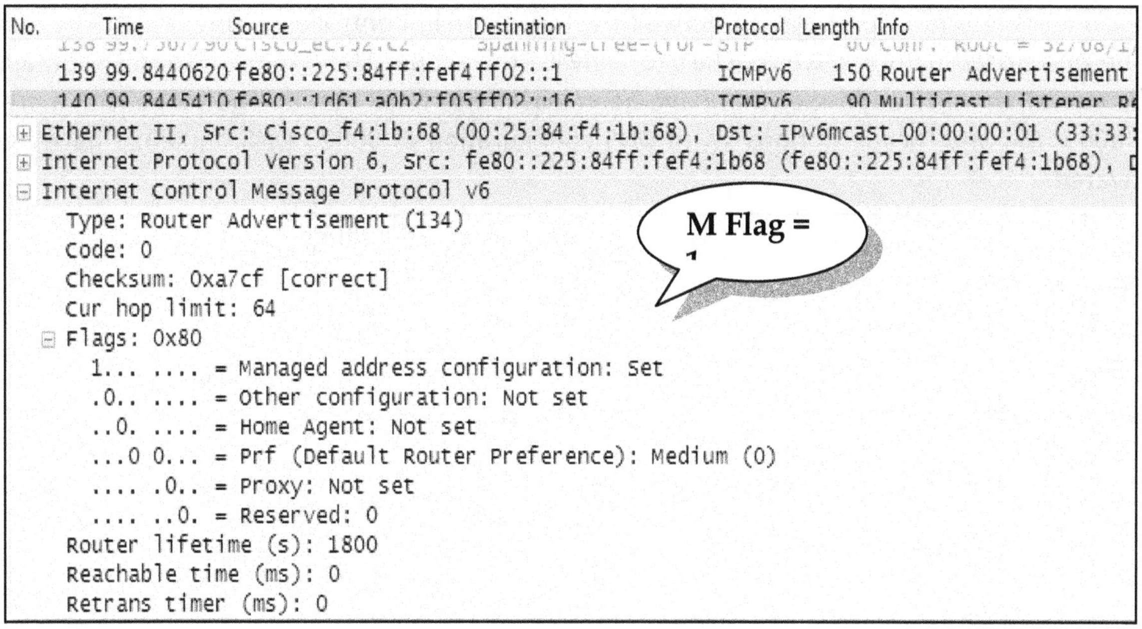

```
No.     Time      Source                     Destination          Protocol  Length  Info
   138 99.7507790 Cisco_ec.92.e2             Spanning-tree-(for-STP        00 Conf. Root = 32/08/1.
   139 99.8440620 fe80::225:84ff:fef4ff02::1                     ICMPv6    150 Router Advertisement
   140 99.8445410 fe80::1d61:a0b2:f05ff02::16                    ICMPv6     90 Multicast Listener R
⊞ Ethernet II, Src: Cisco_f4:1b:68 (00:25:84:f4:1b:68), Dst: IPv6mcast_00:00:00:01 (33:33:
⊞ Internet Protocol Version 6, Src: fe80::225:84ff:fef4:1b68 (fe80::225:84ff:fef4:1b68), D
⊟ Internet Control Message Protocol v6
     Type: Router Advertisement (134)
     Code: 0
     Checksum: 0xa7cf [correct]
     Cur hop limit: 64
   ⊟ Flags: 0x80
        1... .... = Managed address configuration: Set
        .0.. .... = Other configuration: Not set
        ..0. .... = Home Agent: Not set
        ...0 0... = Prf (Default Router Preference): Medium (0)
        .... .0.. = Proxy: Not set
        .... ..0. = Reserved: 0
     Router lifetime (s): 1800
     Reachable time (ms): 0
     Retrans timer (ms): 0
```

M Flag = 1

Figure 95: A network sniffer application indicates an M flag being set.

Router Advertisement M=1; O=0

Part of a resourceful network engineer's work is to scrutinize the RA messages in the network. This methodology is also useful during troubleshooting. Make use of the Wireshark application to activate the "**icmpv6.type == 134**" filter to isolate the RA's messages. Figure 96 is the output *filter* that clearly shows the M flag is active while the O flag is disabled.

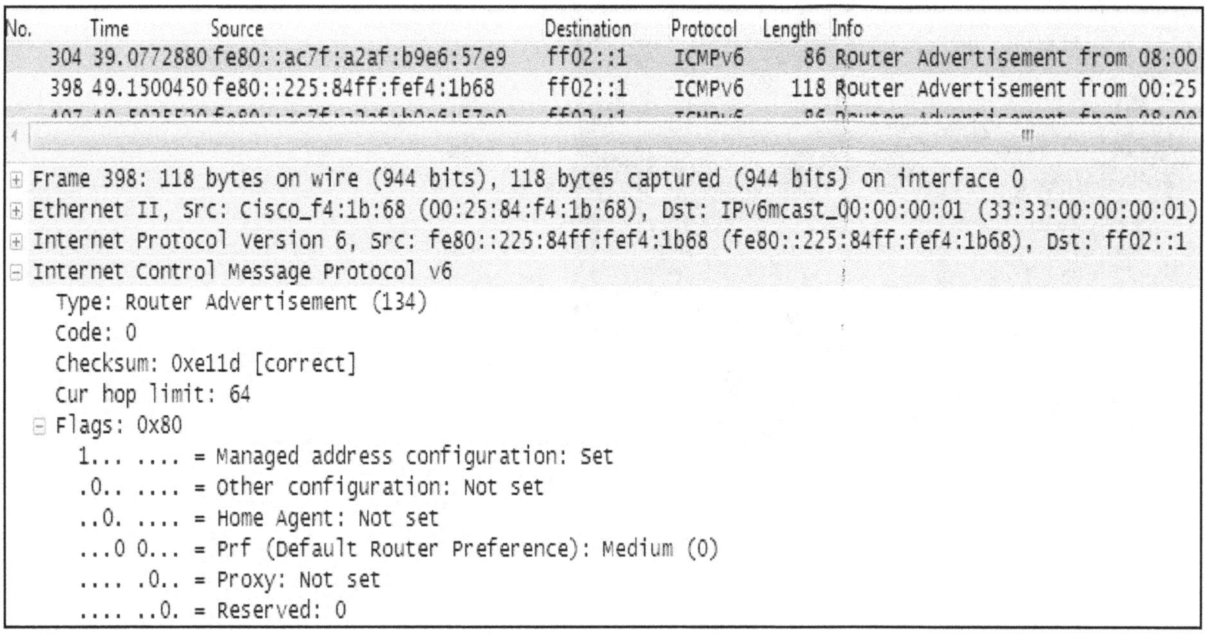

```
No.     Time      Source                     Destination   Protocol  Length  Info
   304 39.0772880 fe80::ac7f:a2af:b9e6:57e9  ff02::1       ICMPv6     86 Router Advertisement from 08:00
   398 49.1500450 fe80::225:84ff:fef4:1b68   ff02::1       ICMPv6    118 Router Advertisement from 00:25
   407 49 5035530 fe80::ac7f:a2af:b9e6:57e9  ff02::1       ICMPv6     86 Router Advertisement from 08:00
◄                                                                                  ⋯     ►
⊞ Frame 398: 118 bytes on wire (944 bits), 118 bytes captured (944 bits) on interface 0
⊞ Ethernet II, Src: Cisco_f4:1b:68 (00:25:84:f4:1b:68), Dst: IPv6mcast_00:00:00:01 (33:33:00:00:00:01)
⊞ Internet Protocol Version 6, Src: fe80::225:84ff:fef4:1b68 (fe80::225:84ff:fef4:1b68), Dst: ff02::1
⊟ Internet Control Message Protocol v6
     Type: Router Advertisement (134)
     Code: 0
     Checksum: 0xe11d [correct]
     Cur hop limit: 64
   ⊟ Flags: 0x80
        1... .... = Managed address configuration: Set
        .0.. .... = Other configuration: Not set
        ..0. .... = Home Agent: Not set
        ...0 0... = Prf (Default Router Preference): Medium (0)
        .... .0.. = Proxy: Not set
        .... ..0. = Reserved: 0
```

Figure 96: **M=1; O=0**

Figure 97 shows that the Windows Server 2012 operating system is configured as a DHCPv6. If the server is also functioning as an Active Directory Domain Controller, then the DHCPv6 needs to be *authorized* before it would start to activate the scope. The "Address Leases" container indicates all the IPv6 addresses that have been leased out to all clients. The scope with a prefix of fa003::/64 and "Scope options" with DNS configuration of 00023 DNS: fa00:3::1 have been activated.

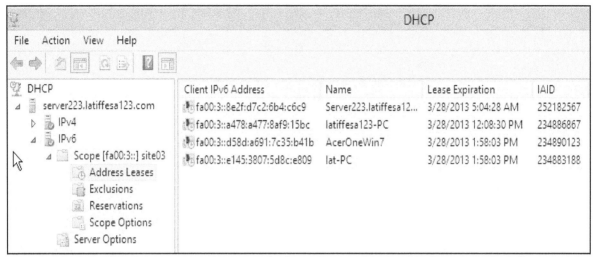

Figure 97: A DHCPv6 server running on Windows Server 2012 with the **M=1; O=0** flag option.

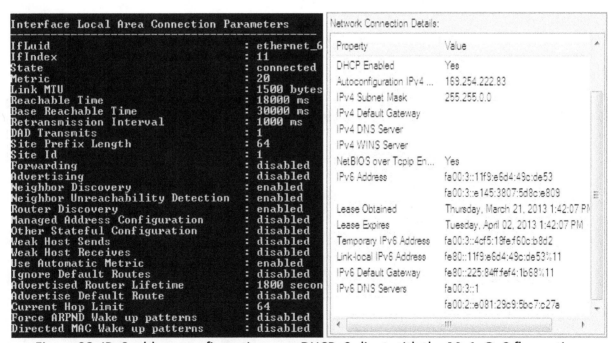

Figure 98: IPv6 address configuration on a DHCPv6 client with the **M=1; O=0** flag option.

The *show interface* command (above, Figure 98) shows the default configuration *default* for "Router discovery" is enabled, "Managed address configuration" is *disabled* and "Other stateful configuration" is *disabled*. Notice that although the DHCP client is configured with "Managed address disabled", the clients would still accept the routers RA to obtain the IPv6 address allocation from DHCPv6 as shown in Figure 97. Note that the address of fe80::225:84ff:fef4:1b68 is the router's address that also functions as the default gateway. The DNS configuration from the DHCPv6, 00023, will function as the preferred DNS Server for the DHCP client.

```
Ethernet adapter Local Area Connection:

    Connection-specific DNS Suffix  . :
    Description . . . . . . . . . . . : Intel(R) PRO/1000 MT Network Connection
    Physical Address. . . . . . . . . : 00-08-74-D2-30-28
    DHCP Enabled. . . . . . . . . . . : Yes
    Autoconfiguration Enabled . . . . : Yes
    IPv6 Address. . . . . . . . . . . : fa00:3::11f9:e6d4:49c:de53(Preferred)
    Temporary IPv6 Address. . . . . . : fa00:3::4cf5:18fe:f60c:b8d2(Preferred)
    Link-local IPv6 Address . . . . . : fe80::11f9:e6d4:49c:de53%11(Preferred)
    Autoconfiguration IPv4 Address. . : 169.254.222.83(Preferred)
    Subnet Mask . . . . . . . . . . . : 255.255.0.0
    Default Gateway . . . . . . . . . : fe80::225:84ff:fef4:1b68%11
    DNS Servers . . . . . . . . . . . : fec0:0:0:ffff::1%1
                                        fec0:0:0:ffff::2%1
                                        fec0:0:0:ffff::3%1
    NetBIOS over Tcpip. . . . . . . . : Enabled
```

Figure 99: IPv6 address configuration on a DHCPv6 client with the **M=1, O=0** flag option.

Figure 99 shows that "DNS Servers" configuration that was there earlier has been flushed out after a system reboot.

Router Advertisement M=1; O=1

No.	Time	Source	Destination	Protocol	Length	Info
122	21.7617700	fe80::225:84ff:fef4:1b68	ff02::1	ICMPV6	118	Router Advertisement
122	22.2038700	cisco_f4:1b:68	cisco_f4:1b:68	LOOP	60	Reply

```
⊞ Frame 122: 118 bytes on wire (944 bits), 118 bytes captured (944 bits) on interface 0
⊞ Ethernet II, Src: Cisco_f4:1b:68 (00:25:84:f4:1b:68), Dst: IPv6mcast_00:00:00:01 (33:33:00:00:00:01)
⊞ Internet Protocol Version 6, Src: fe80::225:84ff:fef4:1b68 (fe80::225:84ff:fef4:1b68), Dst: ff02::1 (ff02::1)
⊟ Internet Control Message Protocol v6
    Type: Router Advertisement (134)
    Code: 0
    Checksum: 0xe0df [correct]
    Cur hop limit: 64
  ⊟ Flags: 0xc0
      1... .... = Managed address configuration: Set ✔
      .1.. .... = Other configuration: Set ✔        STATEFULL
      ..0. .... = Home Agent: Not set                  M = 1
      ...0 0... = Prf (Default Router Preference): Medium (0)   O = 1
      .... .0.. = Proxy: Not set
      .... ..0. = Reserved: 0
    Router lifetime (s): 1800
    Reachable time (ms): 0
    Retrans timer (ms): 0
  ⊞ ICMPv6 Option (Source link-layer address : 00:25:84:f4:1b:68)
  ⊞ ICMPv6 Option (MTU : 1500)
  ⊞ ICMPv6 Option (Prefix information : fa00:1::/64)
```

Figure 100: A network sniffer application indicates an M flag and O flag being set.

Figure 100 shows that both bit M and O have been activated in the router's RA. Both bits are setup to inform all DHCP clients to obtain the IPv6 address and DNS from a DHCPv6 server. The current status "show interface Ipv6" command (Figure 101) shows that the *default* setup for the host has not changed. The host with a hostname of "lat-PC" has obtained both the IPv6 address (Figure 103) fa00:3::33e1:b380:f412:9343 and DNS Servers fa00:3::1. from DHCPv6.

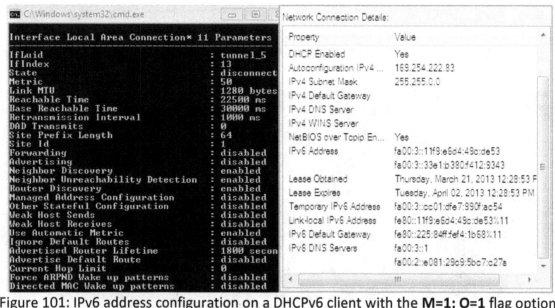

Figure 101: IPv6 address configuration on a DHCPv6 client with the **M=1; O=1** flag option.

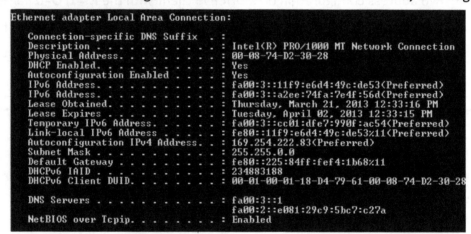

Figure 102: IPv6 address configuration on a DHCPv6 client with the **M=1; O=1** flag option. The DNS server IPv6 address of fa00:3::1 is assigned to the client.

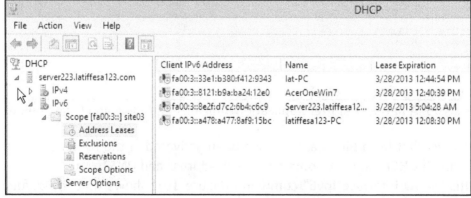

Figure 103: A DHCPv6 server running on Windows Server 2012 with the **M=1; O=1** flag option showing the IPv6 address fa00:3::33e1:b380:f412:9343 of the client.

Figure 103 shows that the DHCPv6 has logged the IP address allocated to the host "lat-PC" as fa00:3:33e1:b380:f412:9343. Figure 104 shows both the DNS configuration on DHCPv6 that is fa003::1 and fa00:2::e081:29c9:5bc7:c27a.

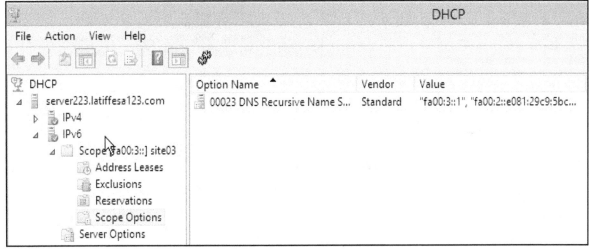

Figure 104: A DHCPv6 server running on Windows Server 2012 with the **M=1; O=1** flag option with the scopes option configured with IPv6 DNS.

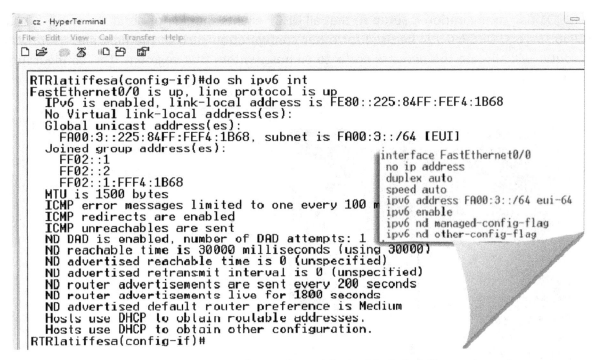

Figure 105: A router configuration with the **M=1 O=1** flag activated.

NOTE: <u>DO</u> ALLOCATE ONE OR TWO MINUTES FOR THE CLIENT TO RENEW ITS IP CONFIGURATION.

Router Advertisement M=0; O=1 (STATELESS)

```
No.      Time       Source                     Destination    Protocol  Length  Info
         26 7.97910100 fe80::225:84ff:fef4:1b68   ff02::1       ICMPv6    118 Router Advertisement from 00:25:84:f4:1b:6

⊞ Frame 26: 118 bytes on wire (944 bits), 118 bytes captured (944 bits) on interface 0
⊞ Ethernet II, Src: Cisco_f4:1b:68 (00:25:84:f4:1b:68), Dst: IPv6mcast_00:00:00:01 (33:33:00:00:00:01)
⊞ Internet Protocol Version 6, Src: fe80::225:84ff:fef4:1b68 (fe80::225:84ff:fef4:1b68), Dst: ff02::1 (ff02::1)
⊟ Internet Control Message Protocol v6
      Type: Router Advertisement (134)
      Code: 0
      Checksum: 0xe15d [correct]
      Cur hop limit: 64
   ⊟ Flags: 0x40
      0... .... = Managed address configuration: Not set
      .1.. .... = Other configuration: Set
      ..0. .... = Home Agent: Not set
      ...0 0... = Prf (Default Router Preference): Medium (0)
      .... .0.. = Proxy: Not set
      .... ..0. = Reserved: 0
      Router lifetime (s): 1800
      Reachable time (ms): 0
      Retrans timer (ms): 0
   ⊞ ICMPv6 Option (Source link-layer address : 00:25:84:f4:1b:68)
   ⊞ ICMPv6 Option (MTU : 1500)
   ⊞ ICMPv6 Option (Prefix information : fa00:3::/64)
```

Figure 106: A network sniffer application indicates that only the O flag is set.

The M0O1 flag configuration is setup so that all DHCP clients should <u>not</u> obtain IP address from DHCPv6 servers. DHCPv6 will be used for other configuration such as the host preferred DNS. The router will allocate the *network* prefix to all hosts within that segment. This configuration setup is known as stateless.

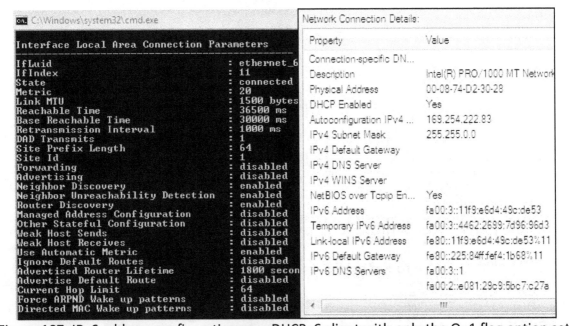

Figure 107: IPv6 address configuration on a DHCPv6 client with only the O=1 flag option set.

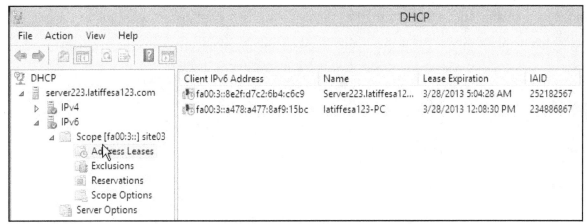

Figure 108: A DHCPv6 server running on Windows Server 2012 with the M=0 ; O=1 flag option set. The host *lat-PC* is <u>not</u> listed in the Address Leases.

Figure 108 shows that the Server 2012 operating system has activated the DHCPv6 service and the address leases does not show any host with the hostname of "lat-PC" which is running Windows 7. This is because bit 0 is activated for the M flag on the router advertisement to all hosts that are in the network segment. In Figure 107, the host "lat-PC" will still obtain the prefix from the router's RA, which is fa00:3::11f9:e6d4:49c:de53. The DNS configuration of fa00:3::1 is obtained from the DHCPv6.

Router Advertisement M=0; O=0

```
No.      Time          Source              Destination   Protocol   Length  Info
   146 18.6754360 fe80::ac7f:a2af:b9e6:57e9   ff02::1    ICMPv6       86 Router Advertisement from 08:00:27:
   334 47.9828430 fe80::225:84ff:fef4:1b68    ff02::1    ICMPv6      118 Router Advertisement from 00:25:84:
   336 48 2050180 fe80::ac7f:a2af:b9e6:57e9   ff02::1    ICMPv6       86 Router Advertisement from 08:00:27:
<                                                                                                        >
⊞ Frame 334: 118 bytes on wire (944 bits), 118 bytes captured (944 bits) on interface 0
⊞ Ethernet II, Src: Cisco_f4:1b:68 (00:25:84:f4:1b:68), Dst: IPv6mcast_00:00:00:01 (33:33:00:00:00:01)
⊞ Internet Protocol Version 6, Src: fe80::225:84ff:fef4:1b68 (fe80::225:84ff:fef4:1b68), Dst: ff02::1 (ff0
⊟ Internet Control Message Protocol v6
     Type: Router Advertisement (134)
     Code: 0
     Checksum: 0xe19d [correct]
     Cur hop limit: 64
  ⊟ Flags: 0x00
       0... .... = Managed address configuration: Not set
       .0.. .... = Other configuration: Not set
       ..0. .... = Home Agent: Not set
       ...0 0... = Prf (Default Router Preference): Medium (0)
       .... .0.. = Proxy: Not set
       .... ..0. = Reserved: 0
     Router lifetime (s): 1800
     Reachable time (ms): 0
     Retrans timer (ms): 0
  ⊞ ICMPv6 Option (Source link-layer address : 00:25:84:f4:1b:68)
  ⊞ ICMPv6 Option (MTU : 1500)
  ⊞ ICMPv6 Option (Prefix information : fa00:3::/64)
```

Figure 109: A network sniffer application with a router advertisement in frame 334.

The M0O0 flag is the default configuration on a router; both the "Managed Address" and "Other configuration" are not activated. The result is all hosts in the network will only generate their link-local addresses. If the router's interface is configured with a global address, its RA will send out a prefix and all hosts in the segment will be configured with an updated global address.

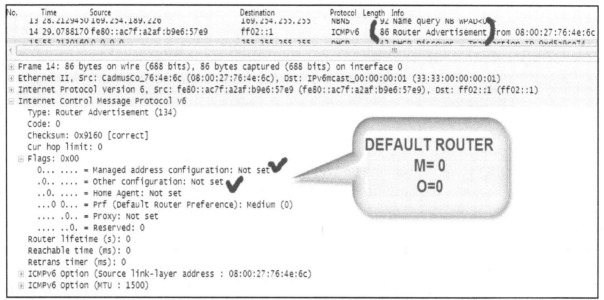

Figure 110: A network sniffer application indicates that the M and O flags is not set (M=0; O=0). The M0O0 setup would not serve any purpose other than:

a. The router's Interface is not activated with GUA or LLA.

b. Transmission RA is simply suppressed on the router's interface.

c.

```
Interface Local Area Connection Parameters      Network Connection Details:

IfLuid                            : ethernet_6    Property                 Value
IfIndex                           : 11
State                             : connected     Description              Intel(R) PRO./1000 MT Network
Metric                            : 20
Link MTU                          : 1500 bytes    Physical Address         00-08-74-D2-30-28
Reachable Time                    : 27000 ms      DHCP Enabled             Yes
Base Reachable Time               : 30000 ms      Autoconfiguration IPv4 ... 169.254.222.83
Retransmission Interval           : 1000 ms       IPv4 Subnet Mask         255.255.0.0
DAD Transmits                     : 1             IPv4 Default Gateway
Site Prefix Length                : 64
Site Id                           : 1             IPv4 DNS Server
Forwarding                        : disabled      IPv4 WINS Server
Advertising                       : disabled
Neighbor Discovery                : enabled       NetBIOS over Tcpip En... Yes
Neighbor Unreachability Detection : enabled
Router Discovery                  : enabled       IPv6 Address             fa00:3::11f9:e6d4:49c:de53
Managed Address Configuration     : disabled      Temporary IPv6 Address   fa00:3::7814:c1db:3e8c:dd3
Other Stateful Configuration      : disabled      Link-local IPv6 Address  fe80::11f9:e6d4:49c:de53%11
Weak Host Sends                   : disabled
Weak Host Receives                : disabled      IPv6 Default Gateway     fe80::225:84fffef4:1b68%11
Use Automatic Metric              : enabled       IPv6 DNS Servers         fec0:0:0:ffff::1%1
Ignore Default Routes             : disabled                               fec0:0:0:ffff::2%1
Advertised Router Lifetime        : 1800 secon
Advertise Default Route           : disabled                               fec0:0:0:ffff::3%1
Current Hop Limit                 : 64
Force ARPND Wake up patterns      : disabled
Directed MAC Wake up patterns     : disabled
```

Figure 111: No IPv6 address DNS Configuration is seen when **M=0 and O=0**.

This setup will only allow the host to communicate within the scope of link-local only. Such configuration would only fit in an organization with a policy that limits the network usage within the scope of local LAN only. This is rarely used.

```
Ethernet adapter Local Area Connection:

   Connection-specific DNS Suffix  . :
   Description . . . . . . . . . . . : Intel(R) PRO/1000 MT Network Connection
   Physical Address. . . . . . . . . : 00-08-74-D2-30-28
   DHCP Enabled. . . . . . . . . . . : Yes
   Autoconfiguration Enabled . . . . : Yes
   IPv6 Address. . . . . . . . . . . : fa00:3::11f9:e6d4:49c:de53(Preferred)
   Temporary IPv6 Address. . . . . . : fa00:3::7814:c1db:3e8c:dd3(Preferred)
   Link-local IPv6 Address . . . . . : fe80::11f9:e6d4:49c:de53%11(Preferred)
   Autoconfiguration IPv4 Address. . : 169.254.222.83(Preferred)
   Subnet Mask . . . . . . . . . . . : 255.255.0.0
   Default Gateway . . . . . . . . . : fe80::225:84ff:fef4:1b68%11
   DNS Servers . . . . . . . . . . . : fec0:0:0:ffff::1%1
                                       fec0:0:0:ffff::2%1
                                       fec0:0:0:ffff::3%1
   NetBIOS over Tcpip. . . . . . . . : Enabled
```

Figure 112: An *ipconfig/all* command revealing the ouput on the client side for the **M=0 and O=0** configuration.

Figures 109- 112 are the output that illustrates the implementation of M0O0 on the local hosts in a network segment where the RA is still issued by the router's *interface* for the prefix of fa00:3.

THE DEFAULT RMO

It is important to identify the current configuration of IPv6 on hosts that will be IPv6 enabled. All three combinations of router discovery (R), managed address (M) and other stateful (O) can be summarized as "RMO". There is the possibility that the IPv6 network project setup was unsuccessful because the *default* value of RMO has been changed without being informed. The following table in Figure 113 can be used as a reference to match the host's setup and the M and O flag on a router. The "*netsh int ipv6 show interface*" command followed by the "*netsh int ipv6 show interface X*" command can be used to determine the current status. Substitute the X with the Idx value from the first command.

DEFAULT	VISTA	WIN 7	WIN 8	Server2012
ROUTER DISCOVERY	Enabled	Enable	Enable	Enable
MANAGED ADDRESS CONFIGURATION	Disabled	Enable	Enable	Disable
OTHER STATEFUL CONFIGURATION	Disabled	Enable	Enable	Disable
NOTE: **WHEN THE ROUTER DISCOVERY CONFIGURATION ON WINDOWS 7 & 8 IS CHANGED TO DISABLE, THE MANAGED AND OTHER WILL AUTOMATICALLY CHANGE TO DISABLE AFTER A SYSTEM REBOOT AND VISE VERSA IF ROUTER DISCOVERY IS ENABLED**				

Figure 113: Summary Table

Router discovery enabled means that the operating system will try to locate a local router within the segment during boot up by sending out a Router solicitation message. If successful the router located will act as a default gateway.

Managed Address disabled means that the operating systems will self generate (autoconfig) its own IPv6 address once it receives a prefix value from a router.

Other Stateful Configuration disabled means the operating system will not activate a preferred DNS configuration.

The following is an example of a router's configuration:

1. **M Bit 1, O bit 0**

   R1(config)#**ipv6 enable**
   R1(config)#**ipv6 unicast-routing**
   R1(config)#int fa0/1
   R1(config-if)#ipv6 nd managed-config-flag
   R1(config-if)#do show ipv6 int fa0/1

2. **O bit 1; M bit 0**

   R1(config)#**ipv6 enable**
   R1(config)#**ipv6 unicast-routing**
   R1(config)#int fa0/1
   R1(config-if)#ipv6 nd other-config-flag
   R1(config-if)#do show ipv6 int fa0/1

```
!
interface FastEthernet0/0
 no ip address
 duplex auto
 speed auto
 ipv6 address 2001:DB8:1::1/64
 ipv6 address FA00:2::/64 eui-64
 ipv6 enable
 ipv6 nd managed-config-flag
!
```

The *"ipv6 enable"* command will activate the IPv6 protocol on the interface. At the same time it will generate a Link Local Address (LLA) based on the EUI-64 format. The next command, *"IPv6 unicast-routing"* will activate the IPv6 routing capability on the local router. This will enable the IPv6 packet to traverse between its interfaces. Such command is configured on the global prompt.

SERVER 2012 DHCPv6 AND ROUTER RA

Figure 114 shows an output from a screen capture. On the front is the output from the terminal of a hardware router showing the time difference between each RA is 200 seconds. At the very same time in the same network there exists a Windows Server 2012 operating system that is also issuing an RA. Both RA messages are seen in the Wireshark application. Under the *Length Info* column there is a Router Advertisement from a different Link local address. Only the host (either router or Server 2012) with the lowest IPv6 address configuration will supercede the other hosts RA in the existing network.

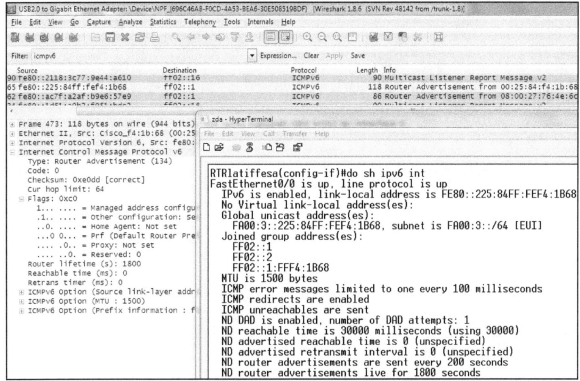

Figure 114: The MAC address 08:00:27:76:4e:6c is Server 2012 while 00:25:84:f4:1b:68 is the router MAC address.

Server 2012 will start transmitting RA once the "netsh int ipv6 set int 12 advertise=enable" is configured on the server. Hosts clients will not be able to activate its default gateway with that only one command being activated. The default gateway configuration will only be accepted by the client once the Windows Server 2012 is configured with the "netsh int ipv6 set int 12 forwarding=enable". The DHCP clients need to be restarted in order to get a consistent result. Refer to Figure 115 for the RA configuration on advertise and forwarding that is configured on Windows Server 2012.

```
C:\>ipconfig /all
   Host Name . . . . . . . . . . . . : Server223 (Server 2012-DHCPv6)
   Connection-specific DNS Suffix  . : latiffesa123.com
   Physical Address. . . . . . . .   : 08-00-27-76-4E-6C
   IPv6 Address. . . . . . . . . .   : 2001:ab8:1234:1::abc(Preferred)
   IPv6 Address. . . . . . . . . .   : 2001:ab8:1234:1:8833:e97a:1170:7ecf(Preferred)
    Link-local IPv6 Address . . . . .     : fe80::ac7f:a2af:b9e6:57e9%12(Preferred)
   Default Gateway . . . . . . . .   : 2001:ab8:1234:1::1
   DHCPv6 IAID . . . . . . . . . .   : 252182567
   DHCPv6 Client DUID. . . . . . .       : 00-01-00-01-18-D5-8F-3A-08-00-27-76-4E-6C
   DNS Servers . . . . . . . . . .   : ::1
```

```
No.   Time      Source                      Destination  Protocol  Length  Info
 78  100.40892 2001:ab8:1234:1::abc         fe80::13 DHCPv6  100 Reply XID: 0x19b/b0 CID: 0001000118d2a31b70
 79  213.63984 fe80::ac7f:a2af:b9e6:57e9    ff02::1  ICMPv6   86 Router Advertisement from 08:00:27:76:4e:6c
 80  217.41061 197.168.2.200               229.255  SSDP     289 NOTIFY * HTTP/1.1
```

```
⊞ Frame 79: 86 bytes on wire (688 bits), 86 bytes captured (688 bits) on interface 0
⊞ Ethernet II, Src: CadmusCo_76:4e:6c (08:00:27:76:4e:6c), Dst: IPv6mcast_00:00:00:01 (33:33:00:00:00:01
⊞ Internet Protocol Version 6, Src: fe80::ac7f:a2af:b9e6:57e9 (fe80::ac7f:a2af:b9e6:57e9), Dst: ff02::1
⊟ Internet Control Message Protocol v6
    Type: Router Advertisement (134)
    Code: 0
    Checksum: 0x50a0 [correct]
    Cur hop limit: 64
  ⊞ Flags: 0xc0
    Router lifetime (s): 0
    Reachable time (ms): 0
    Retrans timer (ms): 0
  ⊟ ICMPv6 Option (Source link-layer address : 08:00:27:76:4e:6c)
    Type: Source link-layer address (1)
    Length: 1 (8 bytes)
    Link-layer address: CadmusCo_76:4e:6c (08:00:27:76:4e:6c)
  ⊟ ICMPv6 Option (MTU : 1500)
    Type: MTU (5)
    Length: 1 (8 bytes)
    Reserved
    MTU: 1500
```

Figure 114a: Server 2012 RA messages type 134 in frame 79

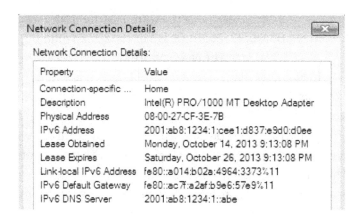

Figure 114b: Host client obtaining the IPv6 address from Server 2012. Notice the IPv6 default gateway is also the Server 2012 IPv6 address.

Figure 115 (next page) can be used as a reference. It shows what happens when combining the DHCPv6 on Windows Server 2012 with and without a router issuing an RA. There are two possible configurations on the host client side: A configuration or B configuration. In the example only A configuration is used.

The C configuration will only enable the DHCPv6 on Server 2012 running on the network without a router. The D configuration enables the DHCPv6 on Server 2012 along with a router issuing RA messages with M0O1 flag. The E configuration enables the DHCPv6 on Server 2012 along with a router issuing RA messages with M0O0 flag. The right most column is the resulting configuration on the host client when the A configuration is enabled.

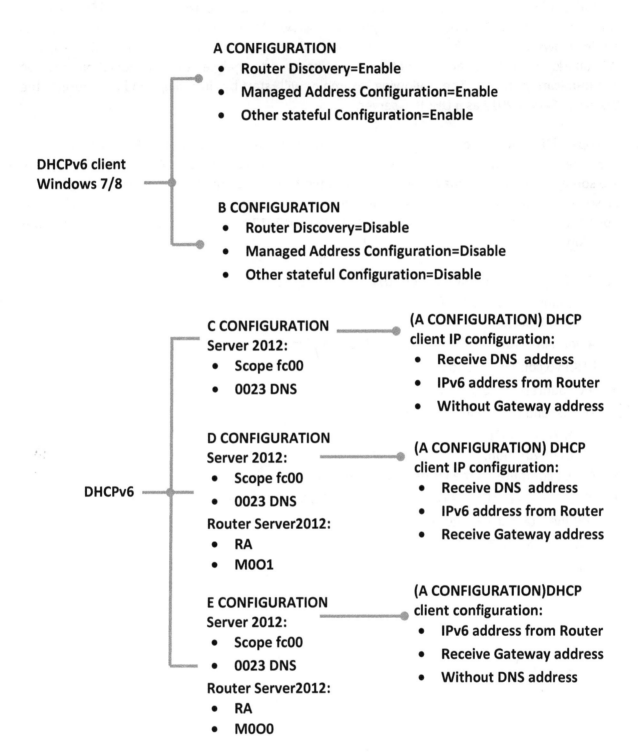

Figure 115: Server 2012 DHCPv6 and Server 2012 Router advertisement

If your test Server 2012 is running on a virtual computer such as the "Oracle VM VirtualBox", configure the VirtualBox network adapters to "Allow All" in promiscuous mode. Promiscuous mode allows transmitted packets to be analysed using a packet sniffer application such as Wireshark. Wireshark allows network engineers to analyse the conversation between communicating hosts. The following example will start by installing and configuring the Windows Server 2012 as a DHCPv6 server.

A scope of IPv6 addresses is created as in Figure 120 to be allocated to DHCP clients and Figure 123 clearly shows that DHCPv6 clients successfully obtained addresses from the scope. There are some addresses that may need to be excluded from the scope for the purpose of future use or some unique devices like IP cameras; these addresses are reserved under the "Exclusions" option as shown in Figure 121. The Windows Server 2012 summary configuration and setup is as follows.

1. The first host: Windows Server 2012
    Hostname: Server223
        Configuration:
*   A domain controller for the latiffesa123.com domain
*   DHCPv6 configured and authorised
*   IPv6 address: fa00:3::1/64 ;   Preferred DNS: ::1
2. The second host: Windows 7 Professional
    Hostname: win7pc
        Configuration:
*   A host computer in the latiffesa123.com domain
*   IPv6 address configuration and Preferred DNS Server: Obtain Automatically
3. DHCPv6 Stateful configuration
*   Scope prefix: fa00:3::/64
*   Exclusion: fa00:3::1
*   00023 DNS: fa00:3::1

Setup Active Directory Server 2012
1. In Server Manager.

2. Add Roles and Features | Next | Role base or feature base installation | Next.

3. Select a server from a server pool | *Highlight* current server | Next.

4. Active Directory Domain services | Add features | Next.

5. Next | Next | Install | Close.

6. Server Manager | AD DS | More | Promote this server to a domain controller.

Server Manager: click on <u>More.</u>

7. Add a new forest | Root domain name: latiffesa123.com | Next.
8. Refer Figure 116.

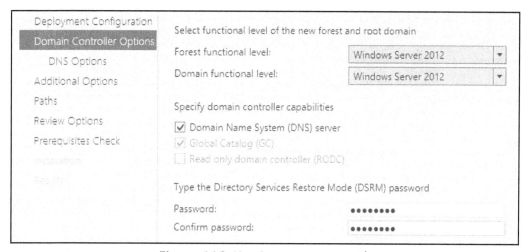

Figure 116: Key in your password.

9. Password: P@55word | Next | DNS options: default | Next | Additional options: default | Next.
10. Paths | Next | Review Options | Next | Prerequisites Check, Install.
11. You are about to be signed off, Close.
12. Login after a system restart.

Verify the Active Directory status
13. Start | Active Directory Users and Computers.
14. Double click latiffesa123.com | Select Users.
15. An Active Directory with an excellent health status will display its organizational units and container. Refer to Figure 117.

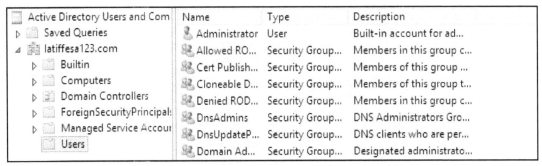

Figure 117: Active Directory Users and Computers.

Installing DHCPv6 Server 2012

1. Server Manager.
2. Add Roles | Next.
3. Role-based or feature base installation | Next.
4. The current server hostname is displayed, server223.latiffesa123.com | Next.
5. DHCP server | Add features.
6. Select Continue | Next | Next | Next | Install.

Figure 118: Feature installation; wait until it's done.

7. Click Close.

Setup DHCPv6 scope and options Server 2012

a. Server Manager | DHCP | More | Complete DHCP Configuration | Next.
b. Authorization: default | commit | summary: Close.
c. Start | DHCP.
d. Refer Figure 119.

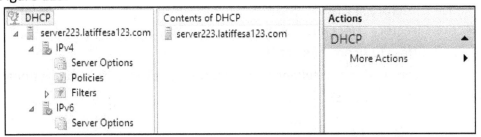

Figure 119: The DHCP service configuration interface.

e. Double click IPv6 | right click IPv6 | New Scope | Next | Name: Scope01 | Next.

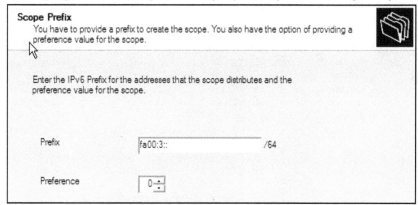

Figure 120: Configuring the DHCPv6 scope.

f. Key in fa00:3:: as the prefix | Next | Add Exclusions: Start IPv6 address: fa00:3::1 and End IPv6 address: <leave blank> | Next.   Refer to Figure 121.

g. The scope that has been activated consists of 18446744073709551429 IPv6 addresses. Refer to Figure 121 for the total number of addresses that are available in the scope being configured. The first IPv6 address will be fa00:3::0:0:0:2 and the last will be fa00:3::ffff:ffff:ffff:ffff.

h.

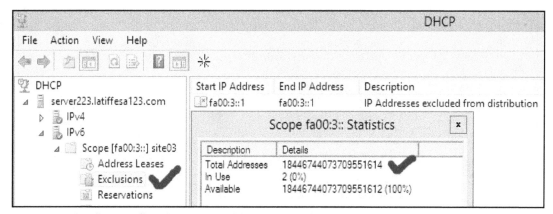

Figure 121: The "In Use" indicates 2 addresses are being leased out and the IPv6 exclusions address.

i. Scope lease: default | Next | Activate scope now: yes | Finish.

j. Double click IPv6 | double click [fa00:3::] scope01

k. Right click scope options | Configure options.

l. Select 00023 DNS Recursive Name Server IPv6 Address List | New Value: fa00:3::1 | Add | OK. The address configured here will be the Preferred DNS configuration for the network.

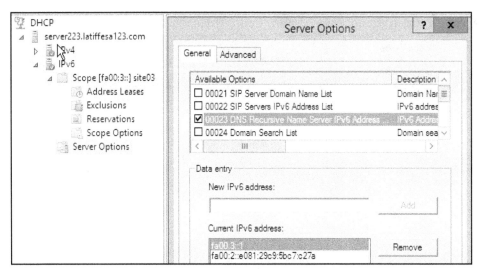

Figure 122: Configuring the 00023 DNS option.

m. Select address leases to identify if there are any hosts had obtained their address configuration from the DHCPv6 server.

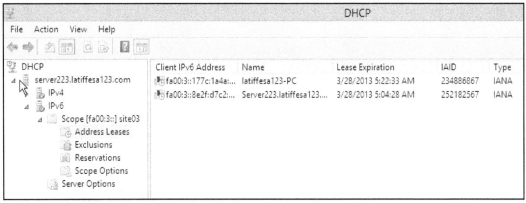

Figure 123: The Address Leases logs active leases.

Verify the Windows 7 Configuration

1. Start | run
2. ncpa.cpl | Enter
3. Right click Local Area Connections.
4. Status | Details | Verify IPv6 address is correct.
5. Configure the Windows 7 operating system to disable the "Router discovery" mode. Use the *"netsh int ipv6 show interface"* command to identify the **Idx** value allocated for the Local Area Connection. Refer to Figure 124. Current status of the Local Area Connection is connected.

```
C:\>netsh int ipv6 show int

Idx     Met         MTU          State                Name
---   --------   ----------   ------------   -------------------------------
  1       50     4294967295    connected     Loopback Pseudo-Interface 1
 11       20           1500    connected     Local Area Connection
 14       50           1280    disconnected  Teredo Tunneling Pseudo-Interface

C:\>netsh int ipv6 set int 11 routerdiscovery=disable
Ok.
```

Figure 124: The ldx values for each interface.

6. The routerdiscovery=disable command will disable the transmission of router solicitation messages on a host. Once it is disable the host will not be able to obtain the IP address of its default gateway.

    netsh int ipv6 set int 11 routerdiscovery=**disable** ← **DISABLE** = Disable IP GATEWAY

- netsh int ipv6 set int 11 managedaddress=enable

- netsh int ipv6 set int 11 otherstateful=enable

7. Verify the current configuration with the ***netsh int ipv6 show int 11*** command.

```
C:\>netsh int ipv6 show int

Idx     Met         MTU          State                Name
---   --------   ----------   ------------   -------------------------------
  1       50     4294967295    connected     Loopback Pseudo-Interface 1
 11       20           1500    connected     Local Area Connection
 14       50           1280    disconnected  Teredo Tunneling Pseudo-Interface

C:\>netsh int ipv6 show int 11

Interface Local Area Connection Parameters
------------------------------------------------------
IfLuid                                  : ethernet_6
IfIndex                                 : 11
State                                   : connected
Metric                                  : 20
Link MTU                                : 1500 bytes
Reachable Time                          : 30500 ms
Base Reachable Time                     : 30000 ms
Retransmission Interval                 : 1000 ms
DAD Transmits                           : 1
Site Prefix Length                      : 64
Site Id                                 : 1
Forwarding                              : disabled
Advertising                             : disabled
Neighbor Discovery                      : enabled
Neighbor Unreachability Detection       : enabled
Router Discovery                        : disabled
Managed Address Configuration           : enabled
Other Stateful Configuration            : enabled
Weak Host Sends                         : disabled
Weak Host Receives                      : disabled
Use Automatic Metric                    : enabled
Ignore Default Routes                   : disabled
Advertised Router Lifetime              : 1800 seconds
Advertise Default Route                 : disabled
Current Hop Limit                       : 0
Force ARPND Wake up patterns            : disabled
Directed MAC Wake up patterns           : disabled
```

Figure 125: Verify the current configuration on the host client.

8. Verify that the Windows 7 operating system obtained all of the configuration from the DHCPv6. The following commands can be used for this purpose.

- ipconfig /release6
- ipconfig /renew6
- ipconfig /all

```
Ethernet adapter Local Area Connection:

   Connection-specific DNS Suffix  . :
   Description . . . . . . . . . . . : NVIDIA nForce 10/100/1000 Mbps Ethernet
   Physical Address. . . . . . . . . : 00-16-D3-0B-B0-92
   DHCP Enabled. . . . . . . . . . . : Yes
   Autoconfiguration Enabled . . . . : Yes
   IPv6 Address. . . . . . . . . . . : fa00:3::177c:1a4a:bd56:e3c3(Preferred)
   Lease Obtained. . . . . . . . . . : Friday, March 15, 2013 10:54:26 PM
   Lease Expires . . . . . . . . . . : Wednesday, March 27, 2013 10:42:06 PM
   Link-local IPv6 Address . . . . . : fe80::a5c2:b004:2fa3:f469%11(Preferred)
   Default Gateway . . . . . . . . . :
   DHCPv6 IAID . . . . . . . . . . . : 234886867
   DHCPv6 Client DUID. . . . . . . . : 00-01-00-01-18-7E-90-62-00-16-D3-0B-B0-92
   DNS Servers . . . . . . . . . . . : fa00:3::1
                                       fa00:2::e081:29c9:5bc7:c27a
   NetBIOS over Tcpip. . . . . . . . : Disabled
```

Figure 126: The client successfully obtained the IPv6 configuration.

9. **Notes:**

a. As of this writing there is no option in the "DHCPv6 option" configuration to include a default gateway IP address to a DHCPv6 clients. The Windows Server 2012 operating system needs to be configured in order to enable it to send out the RA messages.

b. The best practice is to configure a router to advertise RA messages while other IP configurations are given out to clients via the Windows Server 2012 DHCPv6 server.

8. The following is a list of other useful related commands.

- NETSH INT IPv6 SET INT <<interface id/name>> MANAGEDADDRESS = ENABLE
- NETSH INT IPv6 SET INT <<interface id/name>> OTHERSTATEFUL = ENABLE
- NETSH INT IPv6 SET INT <<interface id/name>> ADVERTISE = ENABLE
- NETSH INT IPV6 ADD ADDRESS <<interface id/name>> 2001:DB8::1111
- NETSH INT IPV6 DEL ADDRESS <<interface id/name>> 2001:DB8::1111
- NETSH INT IPV6 SET INT <<interface id/name>> MANAGEDADDRESS=DISABLE OTHERSTATEFUL=DISABLE
- NETSH INT IPV6 SET ROUTE 2001:DB8::/64 <<interface id/name>> PUBLISH=YES
- NETSH INT IPV6 ADD ROUTE <prefix> <<interface id/name>>

DUID

DUID is an acronym for "Device Unique Identifier". There are three categories of DUID:

a. Link layer address + time
b. Vendor assigned unique ID based
c. Link layer address

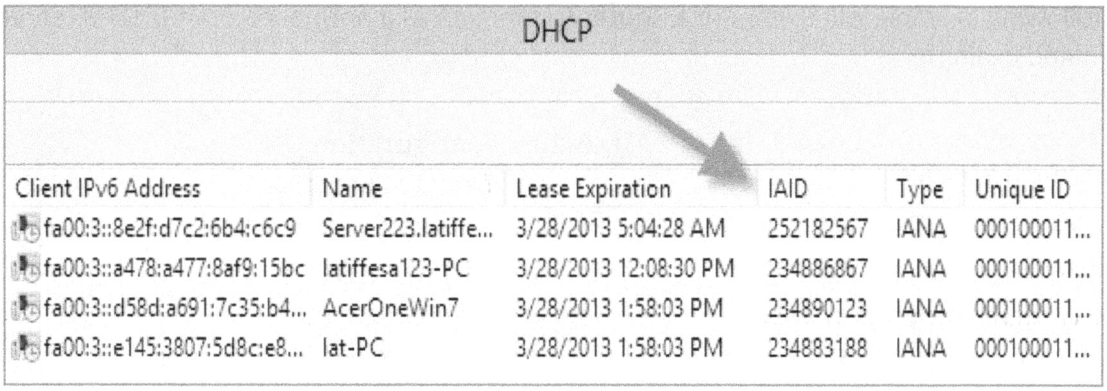

DHCP						
Client IPv6 Address	Name	Lease Expiration	IAID	Type	Unique ID	
fa00:3::8e2f:d7c2:6b4:c6c9	Server223.latiffe...	3/28/2013 5:04:28 AM	252182567	IANA	000100011...	
fa00:3::a478:a477:8af9:15bc	latiffesa123-PC	3/28/2013 12:08:30 PM	234886867	IANA	000100011...	
fa00:3::d58d:a691:7c35:b4...	AcerOneWin7	3/28/2013 1:58:03 PM	234890123	IANA	000100011...	
fa00:3::e145:3807:5d8c:e8...	lat-PC	3/28/2013 1:58:03 PM	234883188	IANA	000100011...	

Figure 127: The IAID value assigned for each interface being logged on the DHCPv6 Server 2012.

The Windows 7 and Windows 8 operating systems will produce its own DUID from category A and B. The "*ipconfig /all*" command will show you the current value of the host DUID and IAID. Refer to Figure 127. DUID is unique for each host while IAID is unique for each host interface. Figure 128 displays the "Identity association identifier" (IAID): 300998385 and followed by the DUID value. Both the combination of DUID and IAID are used as a reference point to allocate an IPv6 address to DHCPv6 clients. It is somewhat similar to an address reservation that is used in IPv4. The Windows Server 2012 operating system makes use of IAID for the same purpose in DHCPv6.

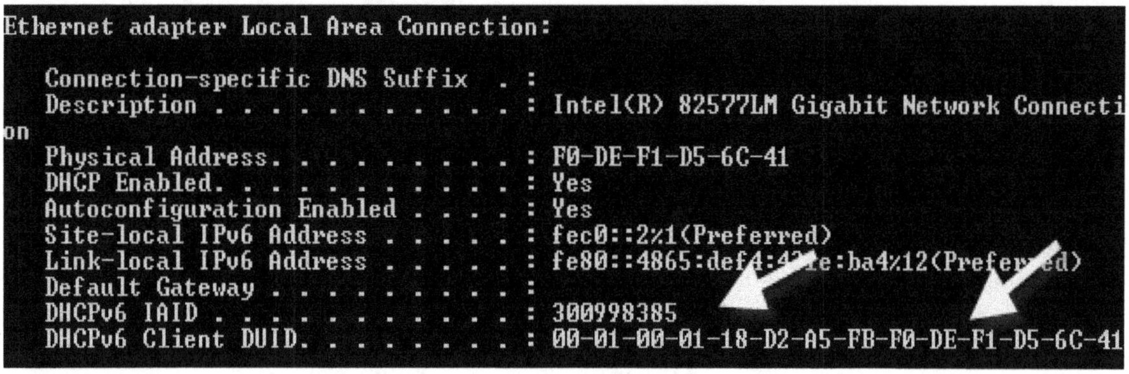

```
Ethernet adapter Local Area Connection:

   Connection-specific DNS Suffix  . :
   Description . . . . . . . . . . . : Intel(R) 82577LM Gigabit Network Connecti
on
   Physical Address. . . . . . . . . : F0-DE-F1-D5-6C-41
   DHCP Enabled. . . . . . . . . . . : Yes
   Autoconfiguration Enabled . . . . : Yes
   Site-local IPv6 Address . . . . . : fec0::2%1(Preferred)
   Link-local IPv6 Address . . . . . : fe80::4865:def4:4??e:ba4%12(Preferred)
   Default Gateway . . . . . . . . . :
   DHCPv6 IAID . . . . . . . . . . . : 300998385
   DHCPv6 Client DUID. . . . . . . . : 00-01-00-01-18-D2-A5-FB-F0-DE-F1-D5-6C-41
```

Figure 128: An IAID value assigned on an interface and an DUID assigned to the host.

STATEFUL ROUTER

A stateful router is a router that functions similar to the stateful DHCPv6 in Microsoft Windows Server 2012 operating systems. The following example will configure a Cisco router to function as a stateful DHCPv6. There are two methods of implementing DHCPv6 on a router. They are:

- Rapid commit
- Normal commit

Rapid commit is a method of communication that depends on exchanging two types of messages, *solicit* and *reply*. Normal commit mode will work by exchanging four communication messages *solicit, advertise, request and reply*. Rapid commit requires that both the client and server (router) be configured as required. .

The following example will configure a Router to function as a normal commit DHCPv6 server. Command example

- configure terminal
- ipv6 *unciast-routing*
- ipv6 dhcp pool <pool name>
- dns-server <address dns server>
- domain-name <domain name>
- exit

Actual configuration:
- configure terminal
- ipv6 *unciast-routing*
- ipv6 dhcp pool latifpool
- dns-server fa00:4::1
- domain-name latiffesa.com

Command example
- configure terminal
- interface <interface name>
- ipv6 address < IPv6 Address>
- ipv6 dhcp server
  <server name>rapid-commit

Actual configuration:
- configure terminal
- interface fa0/0
- ipv6 enable
- no shut
- ipv6 address FA00:3::/64 eui-64
- ipv6 dhcp server latifpool
- ipv6 nd other-config-flag

Verify the current active configuration using the following commands:
- show ipv6 dhcp binding
- show ipv6 dhcp interface

```
RTRlatiffesa(config)#do show ipv6 dhcp interface
FastEthernet0/0 is in server mode
  Using pool: latifpool
  Preference value: 0
  Hint from client: ignored
  Rapid-Commit: disabled
```

Figure 129a: Verifying the pool name *latifpool* is active on the router.

```
Ethernet adapter Local Area Connection:

   Connection-specific DNS Suffix  . : latiffesa.com
   Description . . . . . . . . . . . : Realtek RTL8102E/RTL8103E Family PCI-E Fast Etherne
t NIC (NDIS 6.20)
   Physical Address. . . . . . . . . : 00-23-8B-3A-C4-3C
   DHCP Enabled. . . . . . . . . . . : Yes
   Autoconfiguration Enabled . . . . : Yes
   IPv6 Address. . . . . . . . . . . : fa00:3::2118:3c77:9e44:a610(Preferred)
   Temporary IPv6 Address. . . . . . : fa00:3::f438:6d0f:868:81ee(Preferred)
   Link-local IPv6 Address . . . . . : fe80::2118:3c77:9e44:a610%11(Preferred)
   Default Gateway . . . . . . . . . : ::
                                       fe80::225:84ff:fef4:1b68%11
   DHCPv6 IAID . . . . . . . . . . . : 234890123
   DHCPv6 Client DUID. . . . . . . . : 00-01-00-01-16-DD-D4-95-00-23-8B-3A-C4-3C
   DNS Servers . . . . . . . . . . . : fa00:4::1
   NetBIOS over Tcpip. . . . . . . . : Disabled
   Connection-specific DNS Suffix Search List :
                                       latiffesa.com
```

Figure 129b: The host client successfully obtained the IPv6 configuration.

COMBINATION OF FLAG AND ROUTER DISCOVERY

The combination of M flag and O flag configured on a router and the Windows host operating system configuration of routerdiscovery, managed address and other stateful will produce different results. Figures 130a and 130b were created to simplify and summarize all the possibilities when all of those factors are combined with the result obtained for each configuration combination. From the observation done when the router discovery configuration is changed on the DHCPv6 client, it will also alter the clients configuration of managed other and other stateful.

Such effects will only be seen once a system reboot is done. It is also clear from the observation that if the client's router discovery is disabled, the entire IPv6 protocol will fail to function. The conclusion here is the combined configuration of router and DHCPv6 that is most practical to be implemented is the one shown in reverse-field in Figure 130a.

The following configuration is done on a Cisco 1941 router and DHCPv6 Windows Server 2012. The router activates the M flag using the "*ipv6 nd managed-config-flag*" command. The O flag is also activated with the "*ipv6 nd other-config-flag*" command.

Cisco 1941 Router Configuration:

> Router#configure terminal
>
> Router(config)#hostname latiffesa
>
> latiffesa(config)#ipv6 unicast-routing
>
> latiffesa(config)#int fa0/0
>
> latiffesa(config-if)# ipv6 address 2001:ab8:1234::/64 eui-64
>
> latiffesa(config-if)#ipv6 enable
>
> latiffesa(config-if)#no shut

Note: Address Link Local: FE80::225:84FF:FEF4:1B68

```
latiffesa#configure terminal
latiffesa(config)#int fa0/0
latiffesa(config-if)#ipv6 nd managed-config-flag
latiffesa(config-if)#ipv6 nd other-config-flag
latiffesa(config-if)#end
FE80::225:84FF:FEF4:1B68
```

DHCPv6 Windows Server2012 configuration:

```
IP Add    : 2001:ab8:1234:1::abc;
Gateway: 2001:ab8:1234:1::1; DNS: ::1
Scope     : 2001:ab8:1234:1::;
DNS: 2001:ab8:1234:1::abe
Exclusion:      2001:ab8:1234:1::abc
                2001:ab8:1234:1::abe
                2001:ab8:1234:1::1
```

Figure 130b clearly shows the result obtained once the "routerdiscovery=disable" is configured on a Microsoft Windows 7 and Window 8 operating system. The outcome of such configuration will not produce any result with the possibility of implementation on a common production network today. Each and every host will not be able to make use of the IPv6 protocol. Additionally each host in the network will not be able to obtain other IP address configuration such as default gateway and preferred DNS, which is a requirement for Internet Access. The second row in

Figure 130a indicates that if the configuration of RA, M flag and O flag of the router is enabled and combined with DHCPv6 on Windows Server 2012, Windows 7 acting as DHCPv6 client will successfully obtain IPv6 address from Server 2012, the default gateway address from the router and preferred DNS from DHCPv6 Server 2012. This is known as "stateful DHCP".

The sixth row in Figure 130a indicates that if the router configuration for RA and O flag is enabled together with DHCPv6 running on Windows Server 2012, the DHCP client will obtain an IPv6 address from the router, default gateway address also from the router and preferred DNS from Windows Server 2012. This is known as "stateless DHCP". The router will not log all the IPv6 addresses used by the DHCPv6 clients like a Windows Server 2012 DHCPv6 server would do so using DUID.

WINDOWS 7(SP1)/8 CLIENT. DHCPv6 SERVER 2012 (EN=ENABLE; DIS=DISABLE; ON=ONLINE; OFF=OFFLINE)									
	WINDOWS 7/8			ROUTER		CONFIGURATION WINDOWS 7/8			STATUS	
	Router Discovery	Managed Address "M"	Other Stateful "O"	FLAG "M"	FLAG "O"	Address IPv6 Obtained from	Address Gateway obtained from	Address Preferred DNS obtained from	RA Router Cisco 1941	DHCPv6 Server 2012
1	EN	EN	EN	1	1	Server	NO	Server	OFF	ON
2						Server	Router	Server	ON	ON
3						Router	Router	FEC0	ON	OFF
4						NO	NO	FEC0	OFF	OFF
5	EN	EN	EN	0	1	Server	NO	Server	OFF	ON
6						Router	Router	Server	ON	ON
7						Router	Router	FEC0	ON	OFF
8						NO	NO	FEC0	OFF	OFF
9	EN	EN	EN	1	0	Server	NO	Server	OFF	ON
10						Server	Router	Server	ON	ON
11						Router	Router	FEC0	ON	OFF
12						NO	NO	FECO	OFF	OFF
13	EN	EN	EN	0	0	Server	NO	Server	OFF	ON
14						Router	Router	FEC0	ON	ON
15						Router	Router	FEC0	ON	OFF
16						NO	NO	FECO	OFF	OFF

NOTE:
1. RESTART THE WINDOWS 7/8 TO OBTAIN A CONSISTENT RESULT.
2. IF THE ROUTER DISCOVERY CONFIGURATION IS CONFIGURED TO ENABLE, THE MANAGED AND OTHER CONFIGURATION WILL AUTOMATICALLY CHANGE TO ENABLE.

Figure 130a: Router Discovery, Managed Address and Other stateful enabled.

WINDOWS 7(SP1) /8 X86 CLIENT DHCPv6 SERVER 2012 (EN=ENABLE; DIS=DISABLE; ON=ONLINE; OFF=OFFLINE)										
	WINDOWS 7/8			ROUTER		CONFIGURATION WINDOWS 7			STATUS	
	Router Discovery	Managed Address	Other Stateful	FLAG M	FLAG O	Address IPv6 Obtained from	Address Gateway Obtained from	Address Preferred DNS Obtained from	Router Cisco 1941	Server 2012
1	DIS	DIS	DIS	1	1	NO	NO	FECO	**OFF**	**ON**
2						NO	NO	FECO	ON	ON
3						NO	NO	FECO	ON	OFF
4						NO	NO	FECO	OFF	OFF
5	DIS	DIS	DIS	0	1	NO	NO	FECO	**OFF**	**ON**
6						NO	NO	FECO	ON	ON
7						NO	NO	FECO	ON	OFF
8						NO	NO	FECO	OFF	OFF
9	DIS	DIS	DIS	1	0	NO	NO	FECO	**OFF**	**ON**
10						NO	NO	FECO	ON	ON
11						NO	NO	FECO	ON	OFF
12						NO	NO	FECO	OFF	OFF
13	DIS	DIS	DIS	0	0	NO	NO	FECO	**OFF**	**ON**
14						NO	NO	FECO	ON	ON
15						NO	NO	FECO	ON	OFF
16						NO	NO	FECO	OFF	OFF

NOTE:

1. RESTART THE WINDOWS 7/8 TO OBTAIN A CONSISTENT RESULT.
2. IF THE ROUTERDISCOVERY CONFIGURATION IS CONFIGURED TO DISABLE, THE MANAGED AND OTHER CONFIGURATION WILL AUTOMATICALLY CHANGE TO DISABLE.

Figure 130b: Router Discovery, Managed Address, and Other stateful disabled.

RMO INCONSISTENCIES

A computer network engineer may experience anyone of the following RMO inconsistencies while configuring IPv6 on Microsoft Windows operating systems.

1. **Situation 1**: When the configuration of router discovery is changed from *disable* to *enable*, both the Managed Address Configuration and OtherStateful Configuration will automatically change to enable after several minutes had pass by or after a reboot.

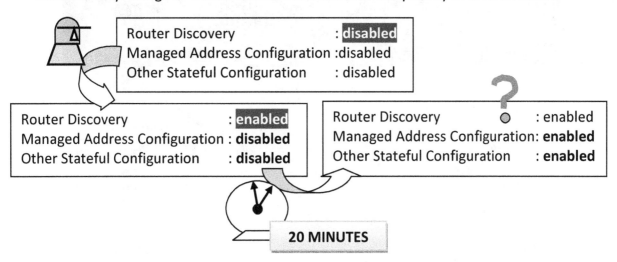

2. **Situation 2**: When the configuration of router discovery is changed from *disable* to *enable*, both the Managed Address Configuration and OtherStateful Configuration will automatically change to disable state after several minutes or after a system reboot. Once this happens, an effort to change the Managed Address Configuration and OtherStateful Configuration to enable will automatically return back the state to disable.

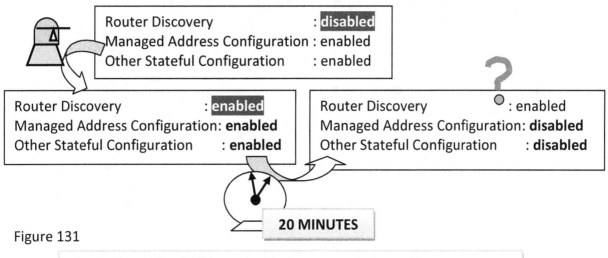

Figure 131

Both situation either 1 or 2 will take place whether the host receives RA messages or not. If the host receives an RA message it will abide by the configuration information in the RA, otherwise it will use the information setup from the DHCPv6 as a last effort.

SLAAC: AN EXAMPLE OF STATELESS ADDDRESS AUTO CONFIGURATION

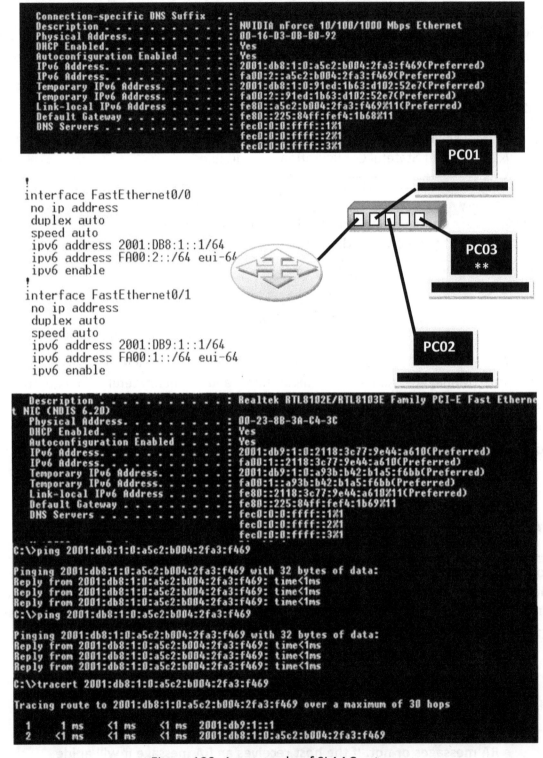

Figure 132: An example of SLAAC setup.

DHCPv6 RELAY

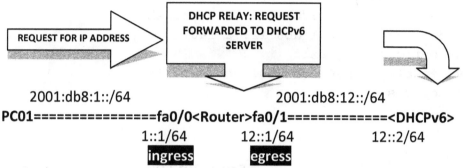

2001:db8:1::/64   2001:db8:12::/64

PC01================fa0/0\<Router\>fa0/1=============\<DHCPv6\>

 1::1/64   12::1/64   12::2/64

[ingress]   [egress]

int fa0/0
ipv6 dhcp relay destination \<dhcpv6\> \<egress\>
ipv6 dhcp relay destination 2001:db8:12::2 fa0/1
ipv6 nd managed-config-flag

Figure: 133: Configuring the DHCPv6 relay on a router.

- Server 2012 DHCPv6: 2001:db8:12::2/64
  o DHCPv6 scope 1: 2001:db8:1::/64 exclusion:2001:db8:1::1/64
  o DHCPv6 scope 2: 2001:db8:12::/64 exclusion: 2001:db8:12::1 & 12:2/64
- Router R1: FA0/0 2001:db8:1::1/64; Fa0/1 2001:db8:12::1/64
- Multicast messages being analysed: ff02::1:2

DHCP relay is a required service in a network environment where a DHCPv6 *server* has been assigned to allocate IP address configuration to all hosts that are segmented across different vlan. This type communication involves the exchange of four DHCPv6 related messages. The multicast used for DHCPv6 communication is ff02::1:2. Such multicast will be isolated within the LAN network. The device router discussed here refers to the layer three switch that is utilized in large organizations. The term *egress* in Figure 133 refers to messages coming out of an interface while *ingress* refers to messages coming into an interface. Refer to Figure 138 which show all four DHCPv6 messages which relate to DHCPv6 protocol. The messages are in message number 236, 239, 240 and 241. The following will explain each message in detail.

a. The router or layer three switch that is configured as a DHCPv6 relay will redirect all DHCPv6 multicast traffic ff02::1:2 coming into its interface of 2001:db8:1::1/64 to the DHCPv6 server DHCPv6 with the address of 2001:db8:12::2/64.

b. The DHCPv6 server will respond with an offer of an IPv6 address and preferred DNS address to be used by the host.

c. Upon receiving the message from the DHCPv6 server the host PC01 will respond with an acceptance message to use the IP address configuration offered to it.

d. The DHCPv6 server will respond with an acknowledgement.

The configuration in Figure 134 will enable the DHCPv6 relay functionality on a router.

- `conf t | ipv6 unicast-routing | int fa0/0`
- `ipv6 enable | ipv6 address 2001:db8:1::1/64 | no shut`
- `ipv6 dhcp relay destination 2001:db8:12::2 fa0/1`
- `ipv6 nd managed-config-flag | exit`
- `int fa0/1 | ipv6 enable | ipv6 add 2001:db8:12:1/64`
- `no shut | end | cop r s`

ROUTER: R1
Fa0/0: `2001:db8:1::1/64`
Fa0/1: `2001:db8:12::1/64`
ipv6 dhcp relay destination 2001:db8:12::2

Server 2012 DHCPv6
IPv6: `2001:db8:12::2/64`
Gateway: `2001:db8:12::1`
Scope1: `2001:db8:1::/64`
Scope2: `2001:db8:12::/64`

PC01
IPv6:
2001:db8:1:0:2118:3c77:9e44:a610
Gateway: fe80:225:84ff:fef4:1b68

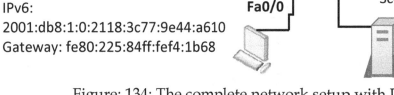

Figure: 134: The complete network setup with DHCPv6 relaying enabled.

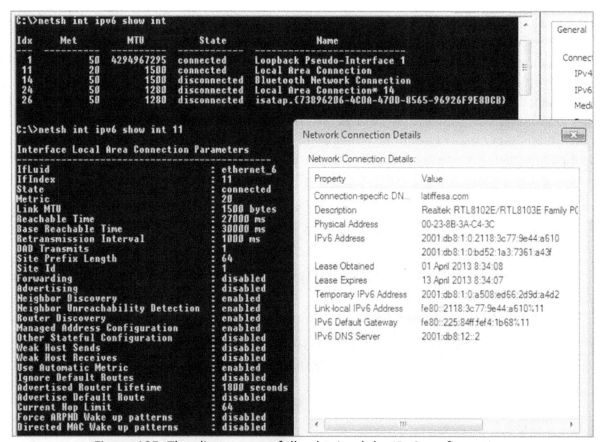

Figure 135: The client successfully obtained the IPv6 configuration.

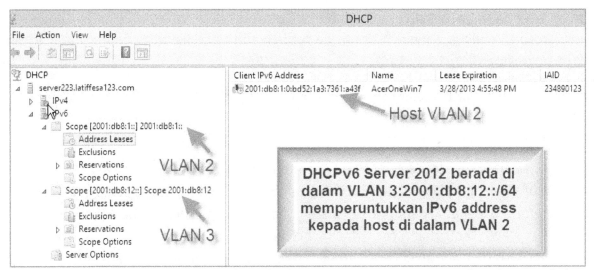

Figure 136: DHCPv6 Server 2012 with multiple scope to support a network with several vlan.

```
RTRlatiffesa(config)#ipv6 unicast-routing
RTRlatiffesa(config)#int fa0/0
RTRlatiffesa(config-if)#ipv6 enable
RTRlatiffesa(config-if)#ipv6 add 2001:db8:1::1/64
RTRlatiffesa(config-if)#ipv6 dhcp relay dest 2001:db8:12::2 fa0/1
RTRlatiffesa(config-if)#ipv6 nd managed-config-flag
RTRlatiffesa(config-if)#no shut
RTRlatiffesa(config-if)#exit
RTRlatiffesa(config)#int fa0/1
RTRlatiffesa(config-if)#ipv6 enable
RTRlatiffesa(config-if)#ipv6 add 2001:db8:12::1/64
RTRlatiffesa(config-if)#no shut
RTRlatiffesa(config-if)#end
```

Figure 137: Router R1 configuration

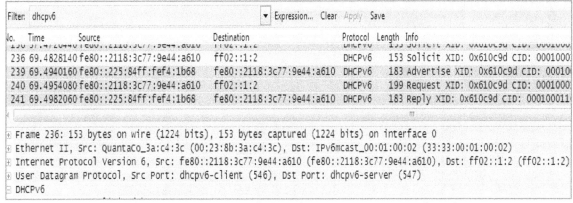

Figure 138: DHCPv6 solicit, advertise, request and reply

The Multicast addresses used in DHCPv6 are:
- "ff02::1:2" (All DHCPv6 relay agents and server)
- "ff05::1:3" (All DHCPv6 Server)

The port numbers used for DHCPv6 are:
- DHCPv6 clients will communicate via UDP port 546
- Server and relay agent will utilize the UDP protocol on port 547

SERVER 2012 AS DHCPv6 & RA

The Microsoft Windows Server 2012 can be configured to act like a hardware router to send out RA messages into the network. Such feature needs to be activated manually with the following commands.

1. Netsh int ipv6 set int 11 routerdiscovery=enabled
2. Netsh int ipv6 set int 11 forwarding=enabled
3. Netsh int ipv6 set int 11 advertise=enabled

The server operating system will start to generate router advertisement messages as shown in frame 20 of Figure 139. The M and the 0 flag can be activated using the *managedaddress* and *otherstateful* command. The RA messages are not a prefix from the unique local address (ULA) category. DHCPv6 clients that receive the RA will be able to activate its default gateway address based on the link local address (LLA). The server which is configured with the fe80::ac7f:a2af:b9e6:57e9 address will transmit RA ff02::1 address messages.

```
No.   Time       Source                    Destination  Protocol Length  Info
18 17.423037 fe80::3efe:c0a8:2cf            fe80::3e ICMPv6   82 Router Solicitation
19 20.053275 fe80::5efe:c0a8:2cf           fe80::5e ICMPv6   82 Router Solicitation
20 23.926721 fe80::ac7f:a2af:b9e6:57e9     ff02::1  ICMPv6   86 Router Advertisement from 08:
21 24.078504 fe80::ac7f:a2af:b9e6:57e9     ff02::16 ICMPv6   90 Multicast Listener Report Mes
```

```
⊞ Frame 20: 86 bytes on wire (688 bits), 86 bytes captured (688 bits) on interface 0
⊞ Ethernet II, Src: CadmusCo_76:4e:6c (08:00:27:76:4e:6c), Dst: IPv6mcast_00:00:00:01 (33:
⊞ Internet Protocol Version 6, Src: fe80::ac7f:a2af:b9e6:57e9 (fe80::ac7f:a2af:b9e6:57e9),
⊟ Internet Control Message Protocol v6
    Type: Router Advertisement (134)
    Code: 0
    Checksum: 0x8998 [correct]
    Cur hop limit: 0
  ⊟ Flags: 0xc0
      1... .... = Managed address configuration: Set
      .1.. .... = Other configuration: Set
      ..0. .... = Home Agent: Not set
      ...0 0... = Prf (Default Router Preference): Medium (0)
      .... .0.. = Proxy: Not set
      .... ..0. = Reserved: 0
    Router lifetime (s): 1800
    Reachable time (ms): 0
    Retrans timer (ms): 0
  ⊟ ICMPv6 Option (Source link-layer address : 08:00:27:76:4e:6c)
      Type: Source link-layer address (1)
      Length: 1 (8 bytes)
      Link-layer address: CadmusCo_76:4e:6c (08:00:27:76:4e:6c)
  ⊟ ICMPv6 Option (MTU : 1500)
      Type: MTU (5)
      Length: 1 (8 bytes)
      Reserved
      MTU: 1500
```

Figure 139: RA messages in frame 20.

Setup:

*   WITHOUT HARDWARE ROUTER
*   WINDOWS SERVER 2012 DHCPv6

Setup B: Server 2012 DHCPv6
Netsh int ipv6 set int 11 routerdiscovery=disabled
Netsh int ipv6 set int 11 managedaddress=enabled
Netsh int ipv6 set int 11 otherstateful=enabled
Netsh int ipv6 set int 11 forwarding=enabled
Disabling router discovery, will automarically disable RA but not vise versa.

Setup A: Server 2012 DHCPv6
Netsh int ipv6 set int 11 routerdiscovery=enabled
Netsh int ipv6 set int 11 managedaddress=enabled
Netsh int ipv6 set int 11 otherstateful=enabled
Netsh int ipv6 set int 11 forwarding=enabled
Enabling router discovery, will automaticallyt enable the M and O flag.

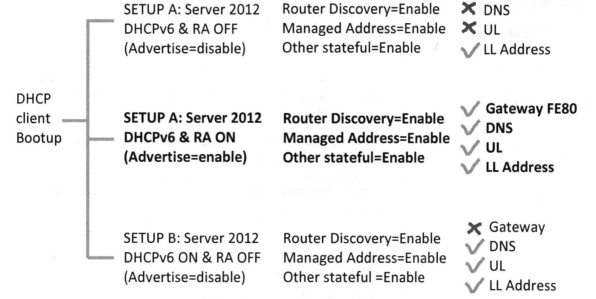

DHCP client Bootup

SETUP A: Server 2012 DHCPv6 & RA OFF (Advertise=disable)
Router Discovery=Enable
Managed Address=Enable
Other stateful=Enable
✗ Gateway
✗ DNS
✗ UL
✓ LL Address

SETUP A: Server 2012 DHCPv6 & RA ON (Advertise=enable)
Router Discovery=Enable
Managed Address=Enable
Other stateful=Enable
✓ **Gateway FE80**
✓ **DNS**
✓ **UL**
✓ **LL Address**

SETUP B: Server 2012 DHCPv6 ON & RA OFF (Advertise=disable)
Router Discovery=Enable
Managed Address=Enable
Other stateful =Enable
✗ Gateway
✓ DNS
✓ UL
✓ LL Address

Conclusion: A Windows Server 2012 DHCPv6 & RA ON will produce the following result.
- The gateway that will be allocated is FE80.
- RA without a prefix.
- The RA will contain the option for M & O flag.

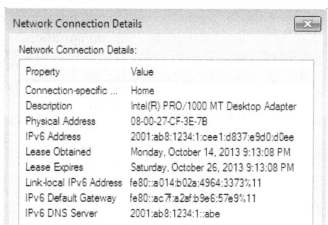

Figure 140

Figure 140 (above) can be used as a guideline in a situation when not even a single router is active in an existing network. The current setup is configured with a Windows Server 2012 acting as a DHCPv6 server in the network. There are two different configuration options configured on the Server 2012: setup A and setup B. The right most column is the resulting configuration on the client for the gateway, dns, UL and LL address. Based on the figure, the preferred setup would be the combination of "setup A" with the RA=ON.

The *netsh* command allows you to activate or deactivate the IPv6 configuration on a host accordingly. Table 141 explains the configuration options.

Usage: set interface [interface=]<string> [[forwarding=]enabled|disabled] [[advertise=]enabled|disabled] [[mtu=]<integer>]

[[routerdiscovery=]enabled|disabled|dhcp]

[[managedaddress=]enabled|disabled]

[[otherstateful=]enabled|disabled]

[[advertisedrouterlifetime=]<0-65535>]

[[advertisedefaultroute=]enabled|disabled]

	CONFIGURATION	EXPLANATION
1	**forwarding**	Allows a packet coming in from an interface to be routed out on another interface.
2	**advertise**	Defines if RA should be advertised out of the current interface. Default is disabled.
3	**routerdiscovery**	Define if the hosts default gateway configuration will be determined by using DHCP.
4	**managedaddress**	Define if managed address configuration is enabled or otherwise. If RA is enabled on this interface this configuration will not take effect. This configuration relates to the router discovery configuration. This configuration determines the host IP address configuration.
5	**otherstateful**	Define if the other stateful configuration is enabled or disabled. If RA is enabled on this interface this configuration will not take effect. This configuration relates to the router discovery configuration. This configuration determines the host preferred DNS configuration.
6	**advertisedrouterlifetime**	Router lifetime. Default is 1800.
7	**advertisedefaultroute**	Define if the current interface will function as a default route.

Table 141: The DHCPv6 client interface configuration option.

Reference
https://www.ietf.org/rfc/rfc3315.txt
https://tools.ietf.org/html/rfc6334
http://www.rfc-base.org/rfc-3315.html
https://tools.ietf.org/html/rfc3315
https://tools.ietf.org/html/rfc4861
http://www.cisco.com/c/en/us/support/docs/ip/ip-version-6-ipv6/113141-DHCPv6-00.html
http://technet.microsoft.com/en-us/library/cc753493.aspx
http://technet.microsoft.com/en-us/library/ee941127(v=ws.10).aspx

Chapter 12
The TCP/IP MODEL

- TCP/IP Model Vs OSI Model
- Network Interface Layer
- Internet Layer
- Transport Layer
  - Connection Oriented Vs Connectionless Protocols
- Application Layer
- Protocol Numbers IPv6

TCP/IP MODEL Vs OSI MODEL

There are two standards that are commonly referred to in computer networking. They are the TCP/IP (Transmission Control Protocol / Internet Protocol) and OSI (Open Systems Interconnection) models. The OSI model is referring to a common standard while the TCP/IP is focused specifically on a networking standard. Both standards are built of many protocols categorised differently at each of their layers based on its working and function. This layer approach allows the standardization of computer related development and compatibility. Additionally the layers introduce a structured method of troubleshooting. As an example, a technical support person would start his troubleshooting from layer one that consists of the cables and connectors. Eventually he will work his troubleshooting to layer two if layer 1 is not the cause of the problem, etc. At layer two the technician will check the health status of the switch which includes its configuration of protocols that is enabled on the switch.

The OSI and TCP/IP models also allow a structured approach for learning computer networks. Referring to Figure 142, this chapter will discuss and introduce the many protocols and standards at each layer, starting at the bottom with the Network Interface layer. Then the chapter will conclude with a brief discussion, with examples, of Protocol Numbers which give direction to transmissions within the network.

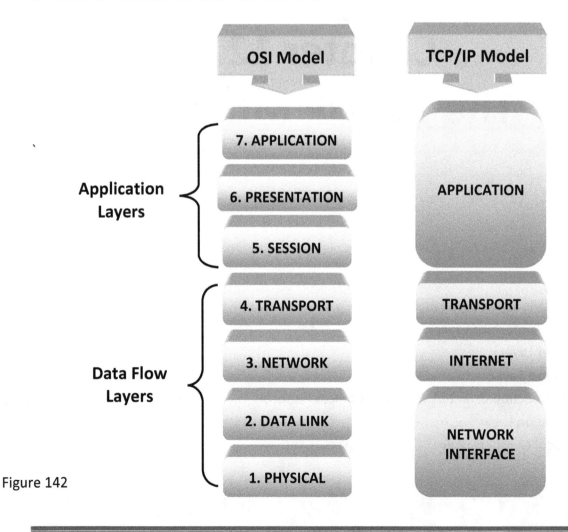

Figure 142

NETWORK INTERFACE LAYER

The Network Interface layer of the TCP/IP model is the equivalent to both the Data link and physical layer combined together in OSI model. Network Interface layer is the first layer of the four layers in the TCP/IP model. The TCP/IP model defines the set of communication rules and formats that a host needs to comply with in order to access a network media. This includes whether the transmission bit needs to be converted to electrical or optical format to match the transmission media installed on the host. The two protocols most commonly related to this layer are Ethernet and Frame Relay. The most widely used network access protocol today is the Ethernet technology. Ethernet utilizes **CSMA/CD** (Carrier Sense Multiple Access/Collision Detection) to access the network medium such as UTP. Network Access *method* defines that a host will monitor the signals on the wire before sending its transmission. If a signal collision occurs, a random time is calculated before the same transmission is sent again. CSMA/CD allows equal rights for any host to access the network medium.

INTERNET LAYER

It is the second layer in the TCP/IP Model. The Internet layer is between the network interface and transport layer. Transmission at this layer is referred to as "IP Datagrams". IP datagrams contains source and destination address. The address at this layer is logical and is known as IP address. Transmission at this layer will travel from one network to the other until it reaches its target destination. There are several protocols at this layer. Some of the protocols at this layer are IP (Internet Protocol), ICMP (Internet Control Message Protocol) and ARP (Address Resolution Protocol). Refer to Figure 143. The IPv6 protocol will only allow fragmentation to happen at the source host. Fragmentation will no longer require an intermediary device such as a router unlike before in IPv4. Fragmentation will take place at the source host Internet layer and once it is completed, it will be passed down to the network interface layer, that is layer one. Fragmentation is required so that the MTU (Maximum Transmission Unit) size can better fit in the path that it is about to use. A larger MTU size will allow more data to be sent in each transmission to the destination host. The benefit of transmitting as much as possible in one transmission will reduce the total number of transmission as a whole. If the transmission path that is about to be used is low in bandwidth, a larger MTU will be a drawback. IPv6 was designed to benefit from the "path MTU discovery" which allows it to identify the most suitable MTU size for the selected path. IPv4 has a predetermined minimum MTU value of 576 bytes, whereas IPv6 minimum MTU size is 1280 byte.

The IP protocol is required for logical addressing, routing, fragmentation and reassembly. The other protocol at this layer, ARP, is required to map a known logical address to a physical address. Today, IPv6 has replaced the ARP protocol with the NDP (Neighbor Discovery Protocol). NDP benefits from multicast communication which is more effective when compared to ARP which depends on a layer two broadcast.

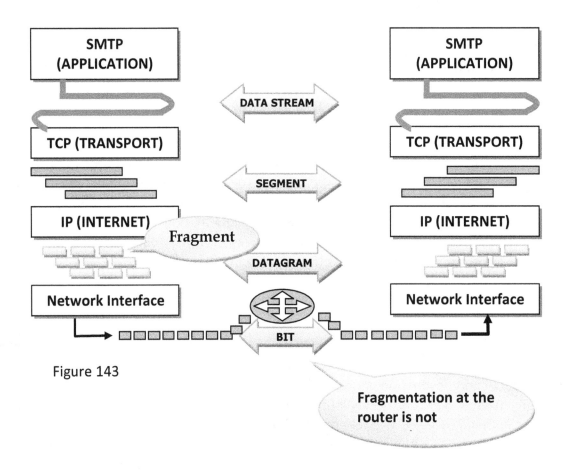

Figure 143

TRANSPORT LAYER

The two well known and main protocols at this layer are TCP (Transport Control Protocol) and UDP (User Datagram Protocol). Each one of these protocols is designed to match the requirement of the application that depends on it. UDP is suitable to meet the requirement of small applications that require speed and performance. DNS is an example of such an application that sends out small amount of signals but requires speed and performance. DNS is a name resolution service that only requires a domain name to be translated to an IP address. It is a type of communication that doesn't take much bandwidth and time.

TCP is commonly used when an application communication requires acknowledgement. Acknowledgement is required especially when the application would send large amount of data. A clear example of this is when a user downloads file from the Internet. If the download was interrupted before it completed, TCP will issue a report in a window, for example, *"download failed, please try again later"*. TCP is a protocol that contains many headers and is meant to support a large continuous transmission. Compared to UDP, the TCP header has more fields in its header. The large number cause TCP to be slower compared to UDP protocol. This weakness is eliminated with the introduction of IPv6 which has a simplified fields compared to IPv4. TCP is categorized as a "connection oriented" protocol where as UDP is "connectionless".

CONNECTION ORIENTED Vs CONNECTIONLESS PROTOCOLS

Connection Oriented: TCP is an example of a layer four (OSI model) protocol that is based on connection oriented communication. UDP being somewhat opposite of TCP, is connectionless. TCP requires that each communication must adhere to an agreed upon set of rules before any session takes place. An example of such agreement is the 3-way handshake. TCP being the upper layer protocol is responsible for the *connection oriented* session at layer four. That means TCP is required to overlook the possibility of communication errors that might occur from layer one up to layer three.

The communication errors referred to above are loss of transmission due to media faults, and receiving hosts that need to receive transmitted data in the proper sequence in order to reassemble it back into valid data. The TCP protocol is used by ftp applications that require connection oriented communications among others. The frame relay protocol is another example of a layer two protocol in the OSI model that is categorized as a connection oriented protocol. Being a Connection Oriented protocol, frame relay will make use of the same path created via virtual circuit. Without virtual circuit there is a possibility that the transmission might use a different *path* to reach the destination. The three stages of connection oriented communications are:

a. **Connection establishment**: Several processes will take place in the background in order to initiate the connection. Among others are the size of *window* and QOS. This is part of a 3-way handshake.

b. **Data Transfer**: The transfer of data will take place at this point.

c. **Connection termination**: Table 144 is a detailed explanation of the entire process of connection termination that was initiated by host PCA (client) to host PCB (file server).

CONNECTION STATUS	EXPLANATION (CONNECTION TERMINATION)
FIN_WAIT 1	PCA sends FIN to PCB and wait for ACK.
CLOSE_WAIT	PCB receives FIN from PCA and sends ACK. PCB waits for the respond from the application.
FIN_WAIT2	PCA receives ACK from PCB and waits for FIN from PCB.
LAST_ACK	The application responded so PCB sends FIN to PCA.
TIME_WAIT	PCA receives FIN and sends ACK to PCB.
CLOSED	PCB receives ACK from PCA.
CLOSED	PCA closes the session gracefully.
NOTE: Use "netstat" to view the connection status	

Figure 144

The following is an example of connection establishment. (Refer Figure 144.)

PCA -------------- SYN --------------> PCB

PCA <------------- SYN & ACK --------- PCB

PCA ------------- ACK --------------> PCB

A connection termination session will follow the three step process.

PCA -------------- FIN --------------> PCB

PCA <------------- ACK & FIN --------- PCB

PCA -------------- ACK --------------> PCB

Today, most connection terminations will make use of the RESET flag instead of the FIN flag. This is because the RESET flag allows faster connection termination compared to FIN flag. The FIN flag will take a longer time to terminate the connection due to the "TIME_WAIT" factor when closing the connection. A connection reset session is as simple as shown here:

PCA<------------- Reset ---------PCB

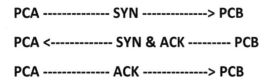

```
No.   Time        Source           Destination       Protocol Length  Info
   8 19.355153 2001:db8:6304::8   2001:db8:6304::9   TCP      82 56181 > microsoft-d  [SYN] Seq=0
   9 19.355189 2001:db8:6304::8   2001:db8:6304::9   ICMPv6   86 Neighbor Advertisement 2001:db8:6
  10 19.355408 2001:db8:6304::9   2001:db8:6304::8   TCP      82 microsoft-ds > 56181 [SYN, ACK]
  11 19.355482 2001:db8:6304::8   2001:db8:6304::9   TCP      74 56181 > microsoft-ds [ACK] Seq=1
```

⊞ Frame 11: 74 bytes on wire (592 bits), 74 bytes captured (592 bits) on interface 0
⊞ Ethernet II, Src: WistronI_d5:6c:41 (f0:de:f1:d5:6c:41), Dst: Ibm_76:ec:c6 (00:11:25:76:ec:
⊞ Internet Protocol Version 6, Src: 2001:db8:6304::8 (2001:db8:6304::8), Dst: 2001:db8:6304::
⊟ Transmission Control Protocol, Src Port: 56181 (56181), Dst Port: microsoft-ds (445), Seq:
    Source port: 56181 (56181)
    Destination port: microsoft-ds (445)
    [Stream index: 0]
    Sequence number: 1   (relative sequence number)
    Acknowledgment number: 1   (relative ack number)
    Header length: 20 bytes
⊟ Flags: 0x010 (ACK)
    000. .... = Reserved: Not set
    ...0 .... = Nonce: Not set
    .... 0... .... = Congestion Window Reduced (CWR): Not set
    .... .0.. .... = ECN-Echo: Not set
    .... ..0. .... = Urgent: Not set
    ....1 .... = Acknowledgment: Set
    .... 0... = Push: Not set
    .... .0.. = Reset: Not set
    ....0. = Syn: Not set
    ....0 = Fin: Not set

Figure 145a: 3 way Handshake (SYN, SYN+ACK, ACK)

```
No.  Time        Source             Destination        Protocol  Length  Info
 24 13.277201 2001:db8:6304::8    ff02::1:ff00:9      ICMPv6    86 Neighbor Solicitation for 2001:
 25 13.277528 2001:db8:6304::9    2001:db8:6304::8    TCP       74 microsoft-ds > 60155 [RST, ACK]
 26 13.277568 2001:db8:6304::9    2001:db8:6304::8    ICMPv6    86 Neighbor Advertisement 2001:db8
```

⊞ Frame 25: 74 bytes on wire (592 bits), 74 bytes captured (592 bits) on interface 0
⊞ Ethernet II, Src: Ibm_76:ec:c6 (00:11:25:76:ec:c6), Dst: WistronI_d5:6c:41 (f0:de:f1:d5:6c:4:
⊞ Internet Protocol Version 6, Src: 2001:db8:6304::9 (2001:db8:6304::9), Dst: 2001:db8:6304::8
⊟ Transmission Control Protocol, Src Port: microsoft-ds (445), Dst Port: 60155 (60155), Seq: 1
    Source port: microsoft-ds (445)
    Destination port: 60155 (60155)
    [Stream index: 0]
    Sequence number: 1   (relative sequence number)
    Acknowledgment number: 1   (relative ack number)
    Header length: 20 bytes
⊟ Flags: 0x014 (RST, ACK)
    000. .... = Reserved: Not set
    ...0 .... = Nonce: Not set
    .... 0... .... = Congestion Window Reduced (CWR): Not set
    .... .0.. .... = ECN-Echo: Not set
    .... ..0. .... = Urgent: Not set
    ....1 .... = Acknowledgment: Set
    .... 0... = Push: Not set
⊞ .... .1.. = Reset: Set
    ....0. = Syn: Not set
    ....0 = Fin: Not set

Figure 145b: Connection Reset (RST+ACK)

Connectionless: UDP (User Datagram Protocol) is a layer 4 protocol (OSI Model) that is categorized as *connectionless*. UDP protocol transmission is known as **datagrams**. *Connectionless* refers to the type of communication where no measures are taken to ensure a dedicated connection exist between two communicating hosts before any data exchange takes place.

OSI MODEL	TCP/IP MODEL	PROTOCOL
APPLICATION	Application	DNS, SNMP, SMTP, FTP, HTTP, X-Windows
PRESENTATION		
SESSION		
TRANSPORT	Transport	TCP, UDP
NETWORK	Internet	IP, IPv6, ICMP, ICMPv6, ARP
DATA LINK	Network Interface	Ethernet, ATM , Frame Relay, V.35
PHYSICAL		

Figure 146

What it means is the transmission will start without taking into consideration if the destination host is active in the network or not. In a well managed network environment where errors are minimized and managed to a minimal level, the use of *connectionless* protocol will work well without any issues. A conversation via *walkie-talkie* is similar to *connectionless* communication where a voice transmitted from a radio *walkie-talkie* will be received clearly or otherwise. If the voice transmission cannot be heard clearly, it will be repeated again. The conclusion here is connectionless communication does not include *error recovery*. Another factor of connectionless communication is the fact that a packet transmitted might use a different path due the fact that no session establishment is made prior to the transmission.

APPLICATION LAYER

The Application Layer is the top layer in the TCP/IP model. The Application Layer functions as an intermediary that provides *service* for any application that requires access to other layers beneath it. The applications itself that is being used is not categorized as any part of the Application Layer. Applications are above the application layer. Included among the many protocols at the application layers are HTTP, SMTP, POP and FTP.

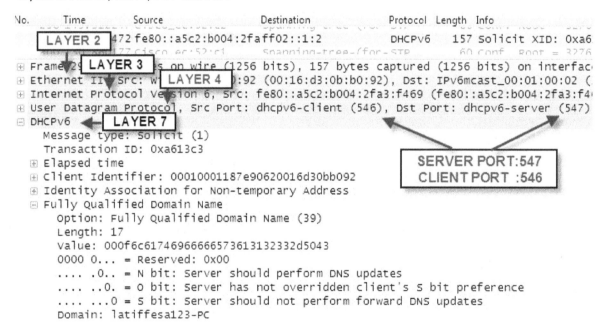

Refer to Figure 147. Every protocol has been allocated a port number so that the purpose of communication can be interpreted by receiving host based on the port number. DHCPv6, being a well known protocol, has been allocated the port number of 546 for client communication and port number 547 for server. It allows both the sending and receiving hosts to understand the purpose of the communication that is about to take place. The Application Layer function is to ensure that the data format that is about to be used can be interpreted by both hosts. Other than that, it defines how the client application on one host communicates with the server application on a different host. As an example, a user that is using a browser might be using several tabs on the browser. Each tab is connected to a *web page* that is actively interactive. The handling of the interactive function on the web page is handled by the application layer on the current host.

PROTOCOL NUMBERS IPv6

The protocol number is used during the communication of two hosts. Much like travelling in a car and making turns at junctions now and then, the same thing actually happens when a computer receives a transmission from the wire. The transmission contains information that's much like a map with the turning points at each junction (at each layer). The protocol number indicates the turning point so that the receiving computer knows which protocol at which layer, and which application will process the request for communication.

Figure 149 shows the process, know as internal routing, that happens within a host itself. Notice that there are two categories of internal communication mapping: 1) port number to protocol and 2) protocol number to protocol.

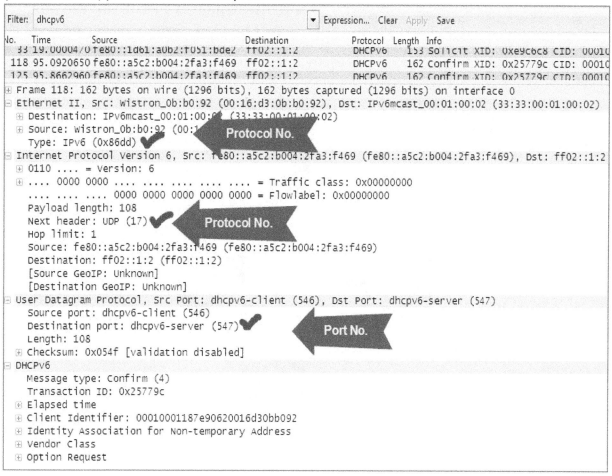

Figure 148

The port number allocated to DHCPv6 is 547 and protocol number for IPv6 is **86dd**. Each and every protocol can be categorized in one of the categories of the TCP/IP Model. Referring to Figure 148, notice that frame number 118 consists of headers Ethernet II, Internet Protocol, User Datagram Protocol, and DHCPv6. It clearly identifies the encapsulation and de-encapsulation processes that happen with the DHCPv6 protocol.

Capturing and analyzing the protocol, protocol number and port number will surely be beneficial when it comes to understanding the computer networking conversations between communicating hosts in depth. For example, configuring a firewall is about opening and closing ports along with specifying the allowed protocol to pass through; which sometimes is referred to based on assigned protocol number. To allow internet access the http protocol needs to be allowed to pass through the firewall, which means that (for example) port 80 needs to open on the firewall.

Troubleshooting a network bottleneck requires the technical support to capture the data traffic traveling through the wires. This data traffic is in raw format and the technical support needs to interpret the raw data. Among the raw data are port numbers and protocols numbers, which the technical support needs to translate to the related protocol. Identifying the protocol number and port number allows the technical support to identify which application is taking most of the Internet bandwidth. Port number 80 relates to the http protocol that is used by a web browser and a protocol number of 1 indicates an ICMP protocol which is used by the ping utility to test a connection or an attacker trying to congest a network.

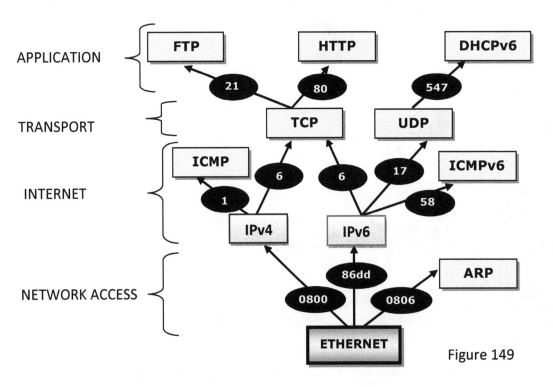

Figure 149

Wireshark is an excellent tool when it comes to *network monitoring* and learning each and every host's communication in a particular network. Wireshark's display is like an essay or a story told about the network being studied or troubleshot. Most of the detailed information displayed in Wireshark needs to be interpreted manually in order to better understand the network or perhaps to fine tune the network by eliminating, reducing, or detecting errors. Each header needs to be scrutinized to view the messages relayed within. Familiarity of the Wireshark protocol filter is certainly useful to better see how the protocols are communicating by filtering only concerned protocols.

The following are some of the filtering examples. Substitute the MAC address, IP address and protocol with the value of interest.

- ipv6.dst == ff02::1:ffa3:f469 || ipv6.dst == ff02::1:fff4:1b69
- eth.src == 00:16:d3:0b:b0:92
- ipv6.addr == ff02::1:ffa3:f469
- icmpv6.type == 135
- tcp.window_size == 0 && tcp.flags.reset != 1
- ! (ip.src == 10.43.54.65 or ip.dst == 10.43.54.65)
- smb || nbns || dcerpc || nbss || DNS
- tcp.port eq 25 or icmp
- ls_ads.opnum==0x09   ..for filtering worm sasser
- eth.addr[0:3]==00:06:5B ..for filtering base on vendor OUI

Reference
- http://www.iana.org/assignments/service-names-port-numbers/service-names-port-numbers.xhtml
- http://www.iana.org/assignments/service-names-port-numbers/service-names-port-numbers.xhtml
- http://www.tcpipguide.com/free/t_InternetRegistrationAuthoritiesandRegistriesIANAIC-2.htm

Chapter 13
MIGRATION

- Planning the Migration
- Transition Technologies
  - ISATAP
  - 6to4
  - Teredo
- GNS3 Freeware Simulator
- Folder Sharing

PLANNING THE MIGRATION

The following are some guidelines for an IPv6 migration project.

3. **Resources:** The migration process really starts with a budget. Enough funds should be allocated and divided into 3 parts for 1) the planning stage, 2) implementation, and 3) contingency – an estimated amount of funds in case requirements arise for the unexpected. The allocation for the planning stage should include the task of identifying the current network status and determining the resources involved in achieving the desired goal. The "unexpected" allocation includes the work force involved to deal with the unexpected. During the implementation stage there is always the possibility of discovering other factors that might not be directly related to the project but ultimately determine if the project will fail or be completed with flying colors. The target for each network engineer is to complete the tasks better than expected.

4. **Project Timeline:** The project duration should be planned based on the project scale to match the resources available. Among factors that should be taken into consideration are hardware delivery delays due to the huge scale requirement of the project itself. Ensure that the time line allocated include other factors such as the possibility to revert back to the original setup and configuration should the need to temporary do so arise. The successful completion of the project will also depend a lot on cooperation from everyone involved directly or indirectly along with the expertise level of personnel.

5. **ISP:** Your local ISP plays an important role in the IPv6 migration project. Talk with your ISP to determine their level of readiness. Once the IPv6 status of your ISP is finalized the related documentation should be prepared and circulated to respective parties. The IPv6 allocation from the ISP to your organization will enable you to structure the IPv6 address hierarchy from top to bottom - which is the end user. An IPv6 address will need to be allocated to network devices and servers. Network devices include routers, switch routers, switches and firewall. Once that is completed, follow with all the servers in the DMZ and *servers* in the LAN.

6. **Response Team:** A select team will need to be detailed to provide support from level one to level three. The team can be comprised of people within the organization, hardware vendors or appointed consultants.
   - Management team: There will be a requirement to handle all the related documents such as licensing, permits and project papers that need to be updated regularly.
   - Support level 1: The support level 1 team will be responsible to setup the project location facilities, equipment and connectivity, equipment safety and cabling. One person from each category should be appointed for this purpose.
   - Support level 2: Members should be comprised of experienced technicians specifically on computer network, hardware, software, operating systems, database and backup. The respective people should be those who are doing the same tasks daily in their organizations.
   - Support level 3: Members in this team are technical experts and consultants with in depth knowledge in their areas. They are team leaders in their units.

7. **Operating System:** Make a list of all operating systems that are categorized as "IPv6 ready". Ensure that each of the IPv6 ready operating systems can fully support all the IPv6 protocol full features. Note that some operating systems that are listed as "IPv6 ready" do not support the full features. Backup all the operating systems that will be configured before any configuration changes are made. Windows 7 and Windows 8 support the imaging features that are really useful for this purpose.

8. **Hosts:** Develop a list of all hosts that are in the existing network. Categorise each host in accordance to its level of importance for the organization's daily function. Such hosts include servers, wireless controllers, firewall, and layer three switches. The three most common categories are public server, private server and computers used by end users.

9. **VLAN:** The total number of VLAN required for the network should be determined clearly. This is a good time to analyze the existing VLAN's effectiveness in fulfilling the existing network requirements. A large number of VLAN would certainly generate too much traffic that will burden the switch processor. The number of hosts per VLAN should be well calculated so that the size of collision domain is at a manageable portion. It should be noted that the maximum amount of acceptable collision is not more than twenty five percent.

10. **Topology:** Once the above is completed, a network diagram of the current network should be produced right away. A network diagram that is too basic would give out a basic impression of the existing network. It is recommended that a detailed physical network diagram be produced that is understandable by everyone involved. This may take a week or more to complete.

11. **Current Status:** Knowledge of the current network issues should be documented prior to implementation, so the project won't be blamed for an already known problem in the network. Each and every issue should be addressed and a workable solution should be agreed upon if the issue would become an obstacle to the current project.

12. **Network Equipment:** The network equipment that will be introduced should be verified and tested in a test environment as a proof of concept. Connectivity from a simulated environment of the end user right to the WAN connection should be evaluated stage by stage. Legacy equipment might have some issues when connected to the latest introduced equipment. Equipment compatibility, operating system compatibility and bugs should be ascertained right from the beginning and solutions to overcome such situations should be finalized and documented for distribution to the technical support staffs. The size of RAM and flash memory for each router and switch should be checked and rechecked. IPv6 is a known protocol that requires huge resources when compared to IPv4. The existing firewall should be checked if it

13. has the capacity to handle the IPv6 protocol that is about to be streamed from the end user computers. The firewall traffic limitations should be clearly outlined.

14. **Folder Sharing:** Setting up folder sharing is different in v6. Please refer to the last section in this chapter for more detail.

15. **Training:** Training on IPv6 should be carried out *before* the project is rolled out and not, as usual, after. This will enable the in-house technical support staff to gain more experience and relate what they have learned in relation to the real world environment.

16. **IPv6 and IPv4:** IPv6 and IPv4 will both be used together during the migration process. This is known as *dual stack*. This means that any network interruption should be minimized and will never effect the entire organization at any one time. The IPv4 address will continue to be used to support legacy applications, though the advantage of using IPv6 will encourage everyone to make the shift sooner or later.

17. **Network Interruptions:** During the migration process there is always the possibility that all network interruptions will be blamed on the project team. Whether the downtime is related or not, the migration project will be the one at fault. Documenting all current networking issues in the organization will help. Assign specific people from the project team to address these known issues should they materialize during the migration.

18. **Classification:** The migration process will need to start from the core network and progress to the desktop computers. Make a list of every desktop computer, and categorized them based on priority level. Priority level can be classified as gold which represent the most critical level, silver intermediate level, and bronze which is the least important. This allows the migration process to move on with the least amount of interruption.

19. **Application:** Make a list of all the applications being used in the organization. Categorise each application base on the level of importance to the organization. Run a test on all the applications starting from the most critical. The IPv4 to IPv6 migration should not cause a major problem to most applications. The applications that will be affected are the ones that are based on "SIP" (Session Initiation Protocol). Some applications that are categorized as SIP are Instant Messaging, Video conferencing, and those that are based on "voice and video over IP". Other applications include the online games.

20. **Dual Stack (IPv4/IPv6 Nodes):** A *dual stack* host is a host that is configured to use the IPv4 together with IPv6. This is the default setup for Microsoft Window 7 and Windows 8 operating systems and Server operating systems such as Windows Server 2008 and Windows Server 2012. Although tunneling will certainly utilize dual stack setup, dual stack itself can be configured to work without tunneling. Dual stack communication between hosts is best explained with the following bullet points:

- If the destination host address is IPv4 then the source host will use IPv4.
- If the destinations host address is IPv6 than the source host will use IPv6.
- If the destination host address is IPv6 embedded IPv4, then the source host will encapsulate IPv6 within IPv4.

The following step will activate dual stack on a Windows machine:
- Click start.
- Search: ncpa.cpl
- Enter.
- Right click Wireless Network Connection
- Properties.
- Select Internet Protocol version 6
- Select Internet Protocol version 4
- Click OK.

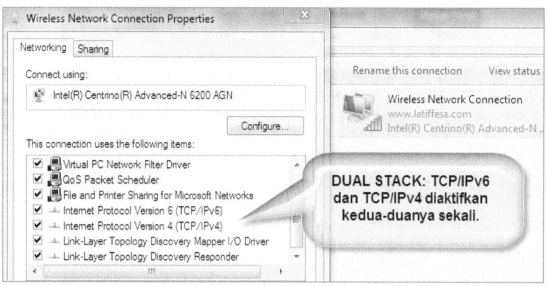

Figure 150

IPv6 TRANSITION TECHNOLOGIES

ISATAP, 6to4, and Teredo are three transition technologies that are designed to assist the transitioning from IPv4 to IPv6. Each is designed to fit in according to existing hardware infrastructure.

- **ISATAP**: A transition technology for LAN implementation. LAN IPv4 to LAN IPv6
- **6to4**: This transition technology is for an IPv6 LAN to IPv6 LAN via an IPv4 ISP WAN connection.
- **TEREDO**: Teredo is meant to be used by an IPv4 LAN hosts via IPv4 NAT accessing an IPv6 WAN.

The sections below will explain each transition technology in more detail. Since the possibility of using Teredo is remote, only a basic introduction to Teredo will be given in this chapter.

ISATAP

The ISATAP (Intra Site Automatic Tunnel Addressing Protocol) technology is meant to be used by LAN hosts. ISATAP will need to be enabled and configured on equipment such as routers. By default, operating systems such as Microsoft Windows 7 and Windows 8 will be able to communicate with ISATAP routers without any additional configuration required. The ISATAP address will be activated only when an ISATAP router is detected by a Windows 7 operating system that is connected to the network. ISATAP is enabled by default on Microsoft Windows Server 2008. The purpose of ISATAP is to enable a direct communication between a host in an IPv4 network to hosts in an IPv6 network. It is an automatic IPv4 to IPv6 translation. The IPv4 host will need to communicate with an IPv6 host via an ISATAP router. The ISATAP router will then connect to the IPv6 host using the link local address fe80. The IPv4 host will find an ISATAP router via DNS. The Router will activate its IPv6 address of fe80::**5efe**:192.168.3.13 (Fe80::5efe:c0a8:30d) as shown in Figure 151 (A hex value of c0a8:30d is equal to 192.168.3.13).

The ISATAP technology can be divided into two usage modes, the *client* mode and the *server* mode. Each client will use the static tunnel to the ISATAP server. The client will then request an IPv6 address. The ISATAP server can be a server operating system or a hardware router. The ISATAP server with its IPv6 address will transmit RA messages that contain information about the current ISATAP configuration to be used by the host. The example in Figure 151 shows a Microsoft Windows 7 operating system acting as an ISATAP client while the hardware router is acting as the ISATAP server. The value of 0000:5efe refers to the usage of the ISATAP technology. The address format of ISATAP is:

64-bit link-local or global unicast prefix + 0000:5EFE + <IPv4 of ISATAP link>

ISATAP Configuration Example:

1. The ISATAP router and the host computer are shown in the figure below:

Windows 7
(ISATAP Client)   (ISATAP SERVER)
PCA ================================= Router
192.168.3.**14**/24   192.168.3.**13**/24
Fe80::5efe:192.168.3.13   2001:db8:22:11::/64 eui-64
                                                          2001:db8:22:11:0:5efe:c0a8:30d
                                                          Fe80::5efe:c0a8:30d

Figure 151

2. Activate the ISATAP feature on Windows 7 (PCA) with the following netsh command.
   a. **C:\>netsh interface ipv6 isatap set state enable**
   b. **C:\>netsh interface ipv6 isatap set router 192.168.3.13**
   c. **C:\>netsh interface ipv6 isatap set router interval=1**
   d. **C:\>netsh interface ipv6 reset**

Note: The command in step "2c" will activate router solicitation on PCA at one minute interval.

3. The boot up process of an ISATAP computer:

 (ISATAP Client)   (ISATAP SERVER)
a. **PCA =====** router solicit **====> fa0/0(Router)Tunnel 0 source fa0/0**

b. **PCA <====5efe & gateway===== fa0/0(Router)Tunnel 0 source fa0/0**

 (ISATAP Client)   **(ISATAP Client)**
c. **PCA ==================> PCB 192.168.3.55/24**
 (ISATAP:IPv6)   **(ISATAP:IPv6)**

Figure 151a

a. PCA activates ISATAP with the "netsh interface ipv6 isatap set state enable" command.

b. PCA send out router solicitation messages in order to connect to ISATAP server.

c. The ISATAP server will than provide the gateway and ISATAP address to PCA.

d. PCA will now be able to communicate with PCB using PCB IPv6 address.

4. The router configuration is shown below:

```
interface Tunnel0
 no ip address
 no ip redirects
 ipv6 address 2001:DB8:22:11::/64 eui-64
 no ipv6 nd ra suppress
 tunnel source FastEthernet0/0
 tunnel mode ipv6ip isatap
!
interface FastEthernet0/0
 ip address 192.168.3.13 255.255.255.0
 duplex auto
 speed auto
```

Figure 152 is the ISATAP configuration on PCA. The configuration allows PCA to obtain the ISATAP gateway from router. The communication from PCA to the ISATAP router can be expedited by reducing the router solicitation interval on PCA to one minute (refer to the netsh command in step 2c). Figure 153 is the configuration on PCB where IPv6 has been disabled. PCB will make use of its IPv4 via ISATAP tunneling address if fe80::5efe:192.168.3.55 and a gateway of fe80::5efe:192.168.3.13 to communicate with PCA is using an IPv6 address of fe80::5efe:192.168.3.14.

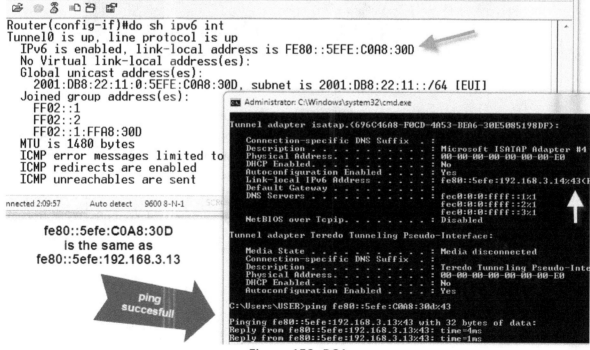

Figure 152: PCA

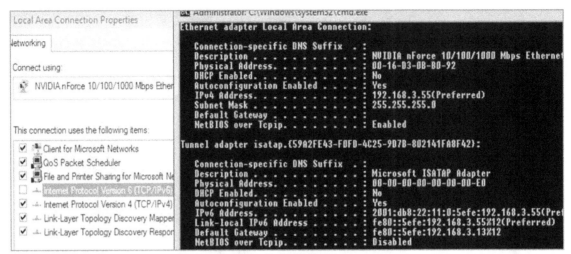

Figure 153: PCB

Figure 153a: PCA(192.168.3.14) ping PCB(192.168.3.55)

6to4

When compared to ISATAP that is enabled on a host computer, the 6to4 technology is a feature that is enabled on a router. 6to4 is an <u>inter</u>-site transition technology whereas ISATAP is an <u>intra</u>-site. The 6to4 technology allows IPv6 networks separated by IPv4 to communicate effectively. A 6to4 router will need to be setup in between both the IPv6 LAN network to communicate via an IPv4 ISP network. The 6to4 is meant as a temporary solution only. An organization that has fully migrated to IPv6 might still have to access a WAN network that still works on IPv4.

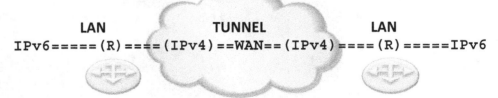

```
      LAN               TUNNEL          LAN
IPv6=====(R)====(IPv4)==WAN==(IPv4)====(R)=====IPv6
```

The ISATAP host which is a router, will be configured with an IPv6 address of 2002:w.x.y.z:SubnetID:InterfaceID, where w.x.y.z is an IPv4 address. The disadvantage of using 6to4 is that only an IPv6 host will be able to connect to an IPv4 host but not vice versa. The acronym 6to4 fits very well with the way the communication works - that is a one way communication from IPv6 to IPv4. The 6to4 configuration example is clearly shown in Figure 154.

THE 6to4 TUNNEL CONFIGURATION

R1
S0/0: 200.1.1.1/24=2002:c801:0101:1::1/64
Lo 0: 2001:db8:6301:ffff::1/64
Fa0/0: 2001:db8:6305:1::1/64

R2
S0/0: 200.1.1.2/24=2002:c801:0102:1::1/64
Lo 0: 2001:db8:6302:ffff::1/64
Fa0/0:m2001:db8:6304:1::1/64

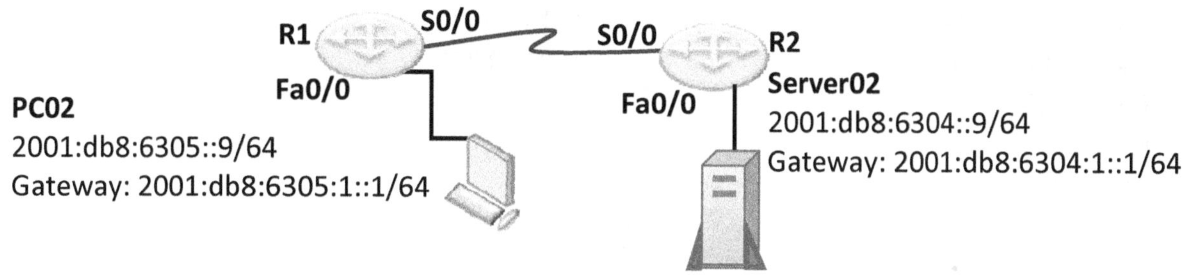

PC02
2001:db8:6305::9/64
Gateway: 2001:db8:6305:1::1/64

Server02
2001:db8:6304::9/64
Gateway: 2001:db8:6304:1::1/64

R1
int tunnel 0
ipv6 address 2002:c801:101:ffff::1/64
tunnel source serial 0/0
tunnel mode ipv6ip 6to4
exit
ipv6 route 2002::/16 tunnel 0
ipv6 route 2001:db8:6302::/48 2002:c801:102:ffff::1

R2
int tunnel 0
ipv6 address 2002:c801:102:ffff::1/64
tunnel source serial 0/0
tunnel mode ipv6ip 6to4
exit
ipv6 route 2002::/16 tunnel 0
ipv6 route 2001:db8:6301::/48 2002:c801:101:ffff::1

NOTE: Ensure that the following commands are configured:
ipv6 unicast-routing
ipv6 enable

Figure 154

Figure 154 is an example of 6to4 network setup that connects a LAN to the ISP. This example refers to an organization that has fully migrated its LAN network to IPv6, though is still connected to an ISP that is based on IPv4. Both router R1 and R2 are connected to each other via interface serial 0/0. The serial interface on R1 is using an IPv4 address of 200.1.1.1 that needs to be converted to an IPv6 address format which is 2002:c801:0101:1::1/64. The IP address of 200.1.1.1 is equivalent to hexadecimal of c801:0101 that is has been integrated into the IPv6 address. Based on this example, the integration of an IPv4 address into an IPv6 address is known as "6to4 address".   On the following page is an example of IPv4 to IPv6 conversion process that leads to the 6to4 address. The example shows that 200 is equivalent to hex C8 and decimal 1 is hex 01. Combine both together we will get a hex value of C801, that is 2002:c801:0101:1::1/64. The value of

":1::1" right after hex 0101 is of any unique value. The loopback interface on the router labeled as "LO" represents any host that is in the LAN behind the router. The loopback interface makes it easy to test the setup without the need to connect an actual physical host to the router. Figure 155 is an example of the *extended ping* utility that allows the ping test to be sent from the loopback interface of the router. Extended ping has the option to ensure that the ping command is sent from the selected source interface, which is the loopback. Without it, there is the possibility that the router will send the ping from any of its interfaces as the source address; then it would not be possible to verify that the test is a hundred percent successful.

IPv4 Address: 200.1.1.1:

200		**1**	
128|64|32|16|8|4|2|1		128|64|32|16|8|4|2|1	
1 1 0 0 1 0 0 0		0 0 0 0 0 0 0 1	
1100 1000		0000 0001	
8+4	8	0	1
12	8	0	1
C	**8**	**0**	**1**

Static routing is used here because most routers on the customer's premises would be utilizing the same type of routing for the reason of reducing the processing load on the router. Two static route configurations were introduced in the router at the global prompt. The static route configuration of "ipv6 route 2002::/16 tunnel 0" is informing the router to support any requests that need to connect to that destination network via the tunnel 0 with the IPv6 address of 2002:c801:101:ffff::1/64.

```
R1
R1(config)#do ping
Protocol [ip]: ipv6
Target IPv6 address: 2001:db8:6302:ffff::1
Repeat count [5]:
Datagram size [100]:
Timeout in seconds [2]:
Extended commands? [no]: yes
Source address or interface: 2001:db8:6301:ffff:1
% Invalid source. Must use IPv6 address or full interface name without spaces (e.g. Serial0/1)
Source address or interface: 2001:db8:6301:ffff::1
UDP protocol? [no]:
Verbose? [no]:
Precedence [0]:
DSCP [0]:
Include hop by hop option? [no]:
Include destination option? [no]:
Sweep range of sizes? [no]:
Type escape sequence to abort.
Sending 5, 100-byte ICMP Echos to 2001:DB8:6302:FFFF::1, timeout is 2 seconds:
Packet sent with a source address of 2001:DB8:6301:FFFF::1
!!!!!
Success rate is 100 percent (5/5), round-trip min/avg/max = 8/107/268 ms
R1(config)#
```

Figure 155

The IP address of 2002:c801:101:ffff::1/64 is mapped to router R1 IPv4 address of 200.1.1.1 on interface serial 0/0. The command "ipv6 route 2001:db8:6302::/48 2002:c801:102:ffff::1" tells the router to use the address of 2002:c801:102:ffff::1 as a gateway to the destination network of 2001:db8:6302::/48.

TEREDO

An organization, whether willingly or not, might choose to continue using the IPv4 protocol for all hosts in the LAN. This means that the network address translation solution such as the firewall may still need to be maintained in order to support connectivity to the Internet. The communication process from an IPv4 host in the LAN to an IPv6 host on the Internet can be explained with the following bullet points.

1. An IPv4 host will first attempt to connect to the Teredo server via the existing NAT device.
2. The Teredo server will then redirect the connection from the IPv4 host to a secondary host that acts as a Teredo relay.
3. Via the Teredo relay, the IPv4 host will connect to the IPv6 host on the Internet.

The entire communication from host to Teredo is based on IPv4. Windows operating systems such as Windows XP and Windows Server 2003 will need to be configured in order to enable the Teredo feature. It's <u>not</u> enabled by default.

GNS3 FREEWARE SIMULATOR

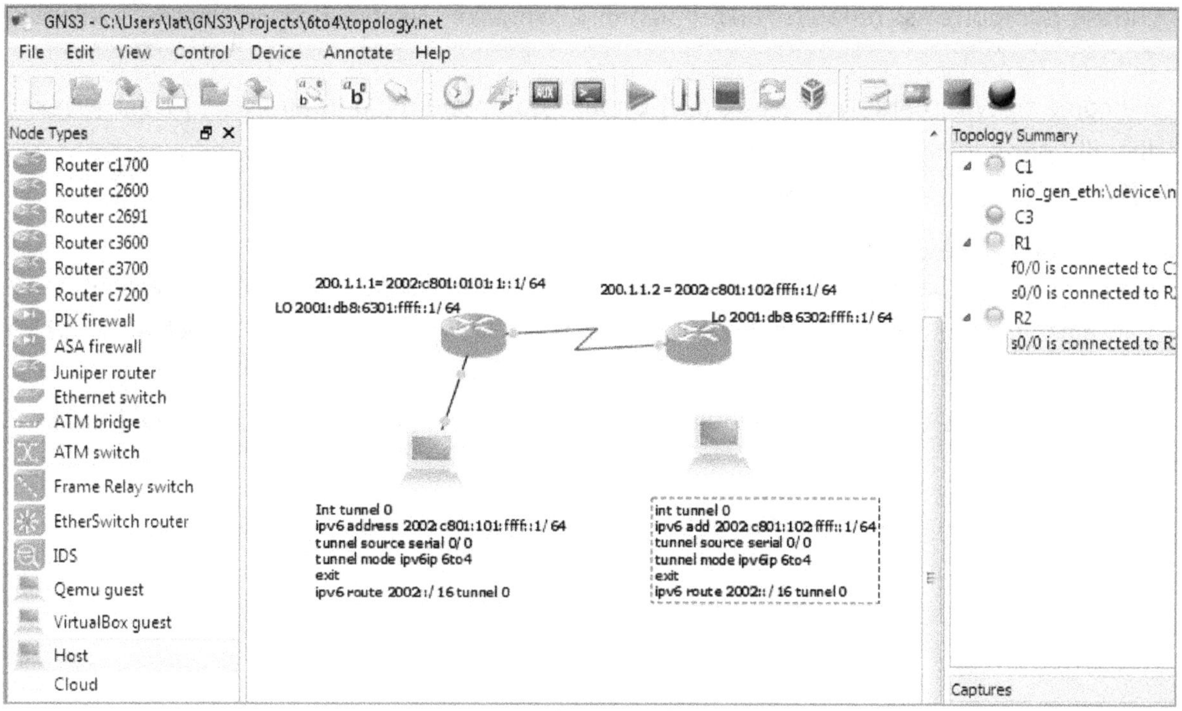

Figure 156

GNS3 is an open source simulator that gives you the option to run IPv6 on simulated network devices. This allows you to save cost from actually buying physical routers and their IOS. Other alternatives such as Cisco Packet Tracer provide the user access to limited commands. GNS3 on the other hand will allow limitless commands as far as you computer processing power can support.

The following are the GNS3 installation steps

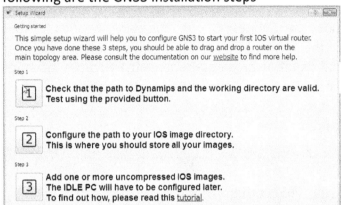

Figure 156a

a. *Download* GNS 3 from www.gns3.net/download.
b. Select GNS3 V0.8.3.1 all-in-one | Select take me to the download site.
c. The installer is GNS3-0.8.3.1 which is 46.6 MB, select save ke Desktop.
d. Double click the installer | Next | I agree | Next | Next.
e. Choose components: default, Next | Install | Winpcap, Next | Next | I agree | Install | Finish.
f. Welcome to Wireshark: Next | I agree | Choose Components: default, Next | Next | Next | Install | Next | Finish | Next | Finish.
g. Refer to Figure 156a |Click Step 1 | OK | Yes.
h. Select Step 2 | OK.
i. Select Step 3 | Setting, Image file, select browse | Point to the *folder* where the that contains the image IOS router 3700, that is image "ipservices" such as c3745-advipservicesk9-mz124-15.
j. The IOS image is compressed, would like to uncompress it? Select Yes | Save | Click on Close.

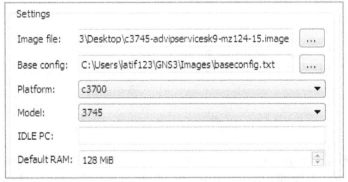

k. Select router 3700 and drag it to the middle of the window.

l. Right click on router R1 selec configure | select R1 | select tab slot | select slot 1 | select NM-4T | click on OK.

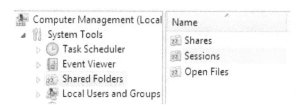

m. Right click R1, select Start | Right click R1, select IDLE-PC | at the windows IDLE PC values, select asterisk | click OK and click Apply |

n. At the *window* IDLE PC value 0x60ba5fe8 has been applied on R1, click OK.

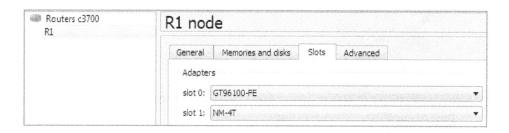

o. Repeat step "K" to "N" for the next router. Than click on "Add a link" at the top left hand side of the windows, hover the mouse on top of the icon to indentify its features.

p. Right click the route | Select Console to start configuring the router.

q. You are now ready to run the GNS3 simulator.

FOLDER SHARING

Folder sharing is a way of file sharing among computers on the network. Folder sharing can be enabled on client operating systems such as Windows 7 and Windows 8 and server operating system such Server 2008, Server 2012 and Linux. Microsoft client operating systems limits the total concurrent connection to only ten sessions. Folder sharing on server operating system are only limited to the processing capability of the server itself. The total number of active sessions can be determined from the "sessions" option with the following steps:

1. Computer | Manage
2. Shared folders | Sessions.

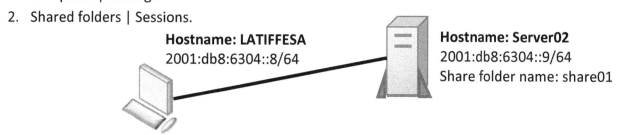

1. Ping <hostname/ipv6 address> to test for connectivity to the host sharing the folder.

```
C:\>ping 2001:db8:6304::9
Pinging 2001:db8:6304::9 with 32 bytes of data:
Reply from 2001:db8:6304::9: time<1ms
Reply from 2001:db8:6304::9: time<1ms
Ping statistics for 2001:db8:6304::9:
    Packets: Sent = 4, Received = 4, Lost = 0 (0% loss), Approximate round trip
times in milli-seconds:   Minimum = 0ms, Maximum = 0ms, Average = 0ms
```

2. Click Start | **\\2001-db8-6304-0-0-0-0-0009.ipv6-literal.net\share01** | Enter. Add the statement ".ipv6-literal.net" after the IPv6 address and replace the":" with "-". Then key in your username and password when prompted.

3.

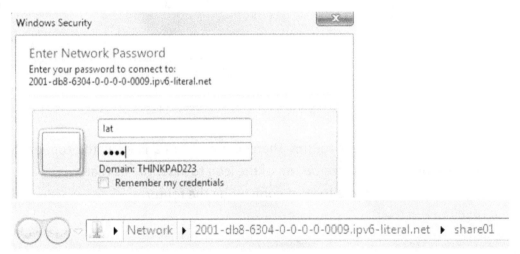

Reference
https://tools.ietf.org/html/rfc5214
https://tools.ietf.org/html/rfc6343
http://www.rfc-editor.org/info/rfc4380
www.gns3.com

APPENDIX

APPENDIX A: Diagram of IPv6 Network Infrastructure
APPENDIX B: Basic Cisco Commands
APPENDIX C: Summary of IPv6 Address Blocks and Usage

APPENDIX A: IPv6 NETWORK INFRASTRUCTURE

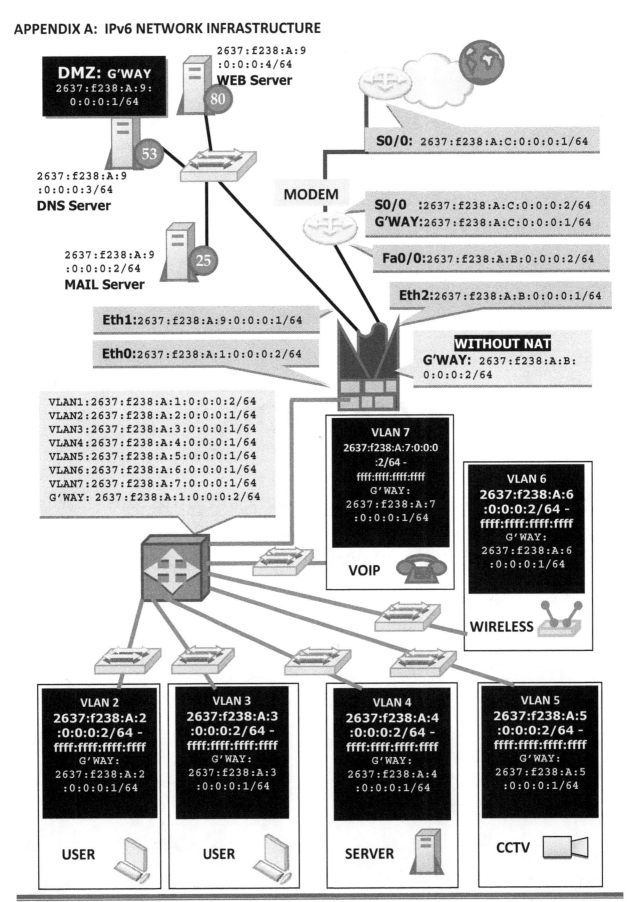

DMZ: G'WAY
2637:f238:A:9:
0:0:0:1/64

2637:f238:A:9
:0:0:0:4/64
WEB Server
80

53

2637:f238:A:9
:0:0:0:3/64
DNS Server

2637:f238:A:9
:0:0:0:2/64
MAIL Server
25

S0/0: 2637:f238:A:C:0:0:0:1/64

MODEM

S0/0 :2637:f238:A:C:0:0:0:2/64
G'WAY:2637:f238:A:C:0:0:0:1/64

Fa0/0:2637:f238:A:B:0:0:0:2/64

Eth2:2637:f238:A:B:0:0:0:1/64

Eth1:2637:f238:A:9:0:0:0:1/64

Eth0:2637:f238:A:1:0:0:0:2/64

WITHOUT NAT
G'WAY: 2637:f238:A:B:
0:0:0:2/64

VLAN1:2637:f238:A:1:0:0:0:2/64
VLAN2:2637:f238:A:2:0:0:0:1/64
VLAN3:2637:f238:A:3:0:0:0:1/64
VLAN4:2637:f238:A:4:0:0:0:1/64
VLAN5:2637:f238:A:5:0:0:0:1/64
VLAN6:2637:f238:A:6:0:0:0:1/64
VLAN7:2637:f238:A:7:0:0:0:1/64
G'WAY: 2637:f238:A:1:0:0:0:2/64

VLAN 7
2637:f238:A:7:0:0:0
:2/64 -
ffff:ffff:ffff:ffff
G'WAY:
2637:f238:A:7
:0:0:0:1/64

VLAN 6
2637:f238:A:6
:0:0:0:2/64 -
ffff:ffff:ffff:ffff
G'WAY:
2637:f238:A:6
:0:0:0:1/64

VOIP

WIRELESS

VLAN 2
2637:f238:A:2
:0:0:0:2/64 -
ffff:ffff:ffff:ffff
G'WAY:
2637:f238:A:2
:0:0:0:1/64

USER

VLAN 3
2637:f238:A:3
:0:0:0:2/64 -
ffff:ffff:ffff:ffff
G'WAY:
2637:f238:A:3
:0:0:0:1/64

USER

VLAN 4
2637:f238:A:4
:0:0:0:2/64 -
ffff:ffff:ffff:ffff
G'WAY:
2637:f238:A:4
:0:0:0:1/64

SERVER

VLAN 5
2637:f238:A:5
:0:0:0:2/64 -
ffff:ffff:ffff:ffff
G'WAY:
2637:f238:A:5
:0:0:0:1/64

CCTV

APPENDIX B: CISCO BASIC COMMANDS

The following table is the prompt and coding for Cisco devices that are commonly used worldwide for network hardware solutions. Certain commands are only available at the respective prompts. Alternatively the *"do"* allows the user to run any command at any prompt. The *show run* command can also be used at the global prompt when used with the *do* command *"router(config)#do show run"*.

		CISCO PROMPT	
	PROMPT	PROMPT	EXPLANATION
1	**USER**	**Router>**	• Most commandS cannot be used here. • This prompts only allows viewing.
2	**PRIVILLEGE**	**Router#**	• The "enable" command will lead you this prompt. • This privilege prompt also means that you are logged in as administrator.
3	**GLOBAL**	**Router(config)#**	• The "configure terminal" command gives you access to this prompt. • This is where general configuration of the router is made.
4	**INTERFACE**	**Router(config-if)#**	• The " interface <int number>" gives you access to this prompt. • This is where interface related configuration is made such as the IP address of the interface.
5	**LINE**	**Router(config-line)#**	• The "line < >" command gives you the option to configure the vty, console and aux.
6	**ROUTER**	**Router(config-router)#**	• This "router < >" command allows you to enable the selected routing protocol.
5	**ROM MONITOR**	**Romon>**	• This prompt is used for disaster recovery and access to it is via the Ctrl+Break key or Ctrl+C. The IOS of the router is replaced at this prompt.

	COMMAND	PROMPT	EXPLANATION
		CISCO CODING	
1	enable	Router>	Access to privilege prompt
2	cop r s		Save current configuration
3	show run		View the current configuration
4	erase start		Delete the startup configuration
5	reload		Reboot
6	show ipv6 int brief		View the interface status
7	show ipv6 route	Router#	View the routing table
8	show controller		Identify if interface is DCE or DTE
9	show version		Identify IOS, Ram and flash
10	debug		Debug current protocol
11	u all		Disable debugging
12	exit		Log out
13	ping		Ping host
14	dir flash		View flash directory
15	hostname		Configure the router's hostname
16	vlan 2	Router(config)#	Create vlan ID 2
17	no vlan 2		Delete vlan ID 2
18	interface		Configure the current interface
19	Ipv6 address		Configure the IPv6 address
20	no ipv6 address	Router(config-if)	Delete the IPv6 address
21	no shut		Activate an interface
22	shutdown		Disable an interface
22	terminal monitor	Router(config-line)	Activate console messages on vty
23	no exec-timeout	Router(config-line)	Disable console auto logout
24	end		Back to privilege prompt

APPENDIX C: A Summary of IPv6 Address Blocks and Usage

USAGE	BINARY	SLASH	EXPLANATIOIN
UNSPECIFIED	**00...0**	**::/128**	The address is 0:0:0:0:0:0:0:0 or :: an IPv6 host address before it is configured with an IP address from a server DHCPv6. It is equivalent to 0.0.0.0 IPv4.
LOOPBACK	**00...1**	**::1/128**	The address of 0:0:0:0:0:0:0:1 or ::1. It is a loopback address equivalent to IPv4 127.0.0.1.
MULTICAST	**1111 1111**	**FF00::/8**	Multicast communication. It replaces the broadcast communication in IPv4.
LINK LOCAL UNICAST (LLA)	**1111 1110 10**	**FE80::/10**	Link Local (LAN). LSB (EUI-64) is derived from the MAC address. It is equivalent to **APIPA** in IPv4.
UNIQUE LOCAL UNICAST (ULA)	**1111 1110 11**	**FC00::/7**	Site Local (LAN).It is used for LAN communication, same at a **private** address in IPv4.
GLOBAL UNICAST (GUA)		**2::/3**	Global (WAN). It is equivalent to the public address in IPv4.

- **::/96** This prefix refers to addresses that are categorised as compatible to communicate with an IPv4 host.
- **::/128** It is an IPv6 address refers to an unspecified address that it is used for internal communication that has not yet receive any IP address from a DHCPv6 server.
- **::1/128** It is a loopback address that is equal to 127.0.0.1 for IPv4. Application that transmits a signal to this destination will receive back its transmission once it is processed by the IPv6 stack.
- **2001:db8::/32** It is an address that is used in IPv6 documentation
- **fec0::/10** It is categorised as "Site-local Address". These addresses should only be used in an internal organization. Anyway it has been deprecated.
- **fc00::/7** It is categorised as "Unique Local Address" (ULA). These addresses can only be routed within the LAN only. It is replaces the site local address. This address uses the 40 bit pseudorandom that is able to avoid an IP address conflict.
- **ff00::/8** This prefix refers to a multicast communication.
- **fe80::/10** It is an address that is categorised as link-local. It is only to be used in a local communication only.